A First Guide to
PHOTOGRAPHY

A FIRST GUIDE TO
PHOTOGRAPHY

Consultant Editors:
JONATHAN HILTON
BARRIE WATTS

Oxford University Press

A Quarto Book

Published by
Oxford University Press, Walton Street, Oxford OX2 6DP

Oxford New York Toronto
Delhi Bombay Calcutta Madras Karachi
Kuala Lumpur Singapore Hong Kong Tokyo
Nairobi Dar es Salaam Cape Town
Melbourne Auckland Madrid

and associated companies in Berlin Ibadan

Oxford is a trade mark of Oxford University Press

A CIP catalogue record for this book is available from the British Library.

ISBN 0 19 910060 8
This book was designed and produced by
Quarto Children's Books Ltd
The Fitzpatrick Building
188–194 York Way
London N7 9QP

ART DIRECTOR Louise Jervis
DESIGN Nigel Bradley
DESIGN ASSISTANCE Eileen Batterberry, Narinder Sahotay, Bernard Nussbaum
MANAGING EDITOR Christine Hatt
EDITOR Mandy Suhr
PICTURE MANAGER Dipika Parmar Jenkins
ILLUSTRATION Julian Baker

PICTURE ACKNOWLEDGEMENTS

Key: a = above, b = below, l = left, r = right, c = centre
Quarto Children's Books would like to thank the following for supplying photographs and for permission to reproduce copyright material. While every effort has been made to trace and acknowledge all copyright holders, we would like to apologize should any omissions have been made.

Ace Photo Agency/Mugshots, page 24cl, cr, bl, br. Rolf Richardson, page 46al. Mauritius, page 46cl. Peter Dazeley, page 46br. Lesley Howling, page 47cl. Gabe Palmer, page 47bl. Ronald Toms pages, 48ar, 62ar. Bruno Zarri, page 48bl. Geoff du Feu, pages 48br, bc. David Kerwin, page 49br. Simone Broadhurst page 51br. Nigel Bradley, pages 13ar, 33cl, 34ar, 39a, 50cl, br, 53al, bl, 59br, 63a, c, 65c, 81br. Paul Forrester/Quarto Publishing plc, pages 3br, 6bl, 10, 15b, 16a, 17cl, br, 18c, 28b, 30b, 36, 83, 84b, 87br. Michael Freeman, pages 25br, 25bl, 51l, 51ar. Fuji Photo UK Ltd, page 14a. C. H Gomersall/RSPB, page 49cr, al. Jeremy Hilder, pages 7c, 18bl, c, 19ac, ar, b, 21b, 22b, 25cl, 26, 27, 29br, 33cl, 43ar, cl, br, 44cr, 45, 52ar, bl, 53ar, al, 58bl, 61bl, br, 62bl, 63b, 64ar, 65al, ar, 66br, 68a, 69a, 71c, b, 72, 73, 75, 80ar, cl. Mrs Margot Melmore/RSPB, page 49c. Helene Rogers, page 35cl. Barrie Watts, pages 14c, b, 15ar, 17a, 19al, ar, 20, 23, 24ar, 25al, ar, 32, 33a, br, 34, 35, 38bl, br, 42, 43al, 44br, 46ar, 54, 55, 56, 57, 58al, ar, br, 59al, ar, bl, 60, 61a, 65b, 66cl, 67a, b, 68b, 69b, 70a, 71ar, 74, 76, 77, 78, 79, 80br, 81a, bl, 84cl, 85, 86.

Front jacket photographs supplied by : Barrie Watts.
Back jacket photographs supplied by: Barrie Watts (above right and left, below left), Jeremy Hilder (centre right), Cannon (centre left).

Manufactured by Eray Scan (Pte) Ltd, Singapore
Printed by Star Standard Industries (Pte) Ltd, Singapore

CONTENTS

GETTING STARTED 10

What is a Camera? 12 – 13

Choosing your Camera 14 – 17

Which Film? 18 – 19

Using your Camera 20 – 21

Composing your Pictures 22 – 23

Natural Light 24 – 25

Flash Light 26 – 27

Developing your Film 28 – 29

Making a Print 30 – 31

Fault Finder 32 – 35

LOOKING AND LEARNING 36

People Portraits 38 – 41

Animal Portraits 42 – 43

Sport and Action 44 – 47

Nature Safari 48 – 49

Photographing Buildings 50 – 51

I Live Here 52 – 53

Photo Story 54 – 55

Holiday Photographs 56 – 59

Landscapes and Cityscapes 60 – 63

Panoramas 64 – 65

Montage 66 – 69

Still Life 70 – 73

Special Effects 74 – 75

Close-ups 76 – 77

Abstract Designs 78 – 79

Self-portraits 80 – 81

DISPLAYING YOUR PICTURES 82

Picture Presentation 84 – 87

Glossary 88 – 91

Index 92 – 93

GETTING STARTED

WHAT makes a great photograph? Read on and find out. In this section of the book, you'll discover everything you need to get started in your new hobby. Learn about the basics of photography and how the camera actually takes a picture. You'll find all the information you need to make the correct choice of camera and film, as well as simple technical explanations that will help you to get the very best out of your camera.

Often the most difficult part of taking a photograph is deciding *how* to photograph the subject you have chosen. This section covers the basic rules of composition, and provides lots of professional tips for creating exciting pictures. When you've finished your film, you can follow the step-by-step guide to developing and printing your own photographs.

Don't forget that the best way to learn is by making mistakes. The simple 'fault finder' at the end of this section will help you to identify exactly where you've gone wrong, so that you don't make the same mistakes again.

WHAT IS A CAMERA?

ALL cameras work in basically the same way. The camera body is a light-tight box. It has a lens at the front and a strip of film at the back that records an image. Light rays are reflected from the object you are photographing and enter the camera through the lens. This focuses the light to project a sharp image of the object onto the film. Inside the camera, before it reaches the film, the light passes through an opening called the aperture. This can be made larger or smaller, to control the amount of light that enters the camera. When you press the shutter-release button, the shutter, a barrier behind the aperture, opens for a timed period. As the shutter opens, the film is exposed to light and an image is recorded.

The combination of the amount of light the aperture allows through, and the length of time the shutter allows it to act on the film, controls what is called the exposure.

THE BIRTH OF PHOTOGRAPHY

For hundreds of years before photography was invented, artists used a drawing aid called a *camera obscura* meaning 'darkened room'. By making a small hole in the wall of a dark room, an upside-down view of the world would be projected onto the opposite wall. This could then be traced on to paper or canvas.

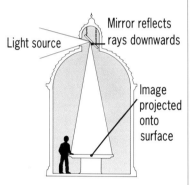

Light source — Mirror reflects rays downwards

Image projected onto surface

An eighteenth century camera obscura *building.*

Eventually, portable wooden *camera obscuras* were made and these looked a lot like cameras today.

In 1826, a Frenchman called Nicéphore Niépce used this principle to produce the first permanent images using the direct action of light.

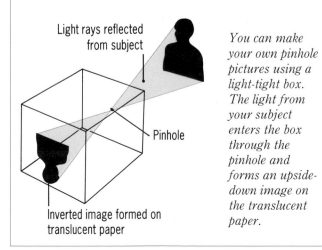

Light rays reflected from subject

Pinhole

Inverted image formed on translucent paper

You can make your own pinhole pictures using a light-tight box. The light from your subject enters the box through the pinhole and forms an upside-down image on the translucent paper.

Film cassette
This contains the roll of unexposed film.

Viewfinder
This 'window' lets you view your subject as it will appear in your picture.

Film image
The light forms an upside-down image on the film. Film is made from a transparent plastic strip coated with chemicals called silver salts (compounds of silver). The silver salts change chemically when light falls on them, and in doing so, record the pattern of reflected light coming from the subject.

Take-up spool
Exposed film is wound onto the spool after each picture has been taken. When all the frames have been exposed, the whole film is rewound back into the cassette and can be removed from the camera for processing.

LOOK IT UP!

Viewfinder	p 21
Shutter speed	p 21
Lens aperture	p 21

Lens
Light enters the camera through the lens. The lens is a combination of specially shaped pieces of glass that bend, or refract, the light to form a sharp, focused image on the film.

Light rays
Light rays are reflected from an object and enter the camera through the lens.

Aperture
The light passes through the aperture, a hole behind the camera lens. A circle of moveable metal blades makes the hole larger or smaller. This controls how much light enters the camera, so giving different amounts of exposure to the film. On simple cameras this is fixed at one size. On more complex cameras it can be adjusted. The aperture size may be controlled automatically or manually.

Shutter
The shutter opens when you press the shutter-release button, allowing light to reach the film. This controls when and for how long light is allowed to act on the film. Together with the size of the aperture, it determines the film exposure. The shutter is controlled either automatically, or by turning the shutter speed dial on a manual camera.

Automatic film transport
A small motorized mechanism winds the film from cassette to spool and back again.

Changing views
With a compact camera, you look through a viewfinder window that is above and to one side of the lens. This means that there is a slight difference between what the viewfinder and the lens see. The SLR (single lens reflex) camera is different. Inside the SLR, a mirror angled at 45° reflects light from the lens up and out through the rear viewfinder window. This means that you always share exactly the same view as the lens, no matter what lens is used. When you press the shutter-release button, the mirror flips up out of the way and the shutter opens, allowing light to reach the film.

SLR viewing system

Viewing your subject – shutter closed

Pentaprism

Angled mirror

Mirror flips up and light reaches film

Light from subject

Photographing your subject – shutter open

Film records image

Light from subject

CHOOSING YOUR CAMERA

CHOOSING a camera can be a very confusing business! There are many different types and designs, all offering different features. They range from the simplest 'point and shoot' cameras to very sophisticated models that are totally automatic, and even computerized. On the next few pages you will find a guide to the sorts of cameras that are available, starting with the least expensive, and an explanation of some of the most common features.

Fixed-focus
This means that the lens cannot be altered to focus on subjects at different distances from the camera. It is preset so that everything from a few metres in front of the camera will be in focus.

Autofocus
This feature allows the camera lens to move in and out to focus automatically on any subject that you place in the target area of the viewfinder. You can focus on subjects closer to you than is possible with a fixed-focus camera.

Autoexposure
This means that the camera has a tiny cell that is sensitive to light falling on it from the subject. This cell automatically alters the aperture size or shutter speed, so the film receives the right amount of light for correct exposure.

Automatic film transport
This means that the camera has a tiny motor that automatically winds the film on to its start position when you shut the back. It positions a fresh piece of film every time you take a picture, and then rewinds the film back into the cassette.

110 cameras
These are simple, inexpensive cameras that have no controls, apart from the shutter-release button. Film comes in a drop-in cartridge. Each negative is very small and so enlargements can be poor quality.

Shutter-release button — Viewfinder — Lens

Shutter-release button — Viewfinder — Built-in flash — Lens

● *Fixed focus*

● *Simple autoexposure*

● *Built-in flash*

Shutter-release button — Viewfinder — Built-in flash — Lens cover control — Lens

Disposable 35 mm cameras

These are fun cameras with no controls, but they come loaded with 35 mm film and so give better-quality prints. When you have taken the last shot, you send the whole camera away to process the film. Some models are waterproof or take long thin photographs called panoramas.

● *Fixed focus*

● *Simple autoexposure*

● *Built-in flash*

Simple 35 mm compact cameras

These take much better-quality pictures than either a 110 or a disposable camera and allow you to change the speed of film that you use to compensate for bright or dim lighting conditions. These are easy to use cameras, ideal for quick 'point and shoot' photographs.

● *Simple autoexposure*

● *Fixed focus*

● *Built-in flash*

Sophisticated 35 mm compact cameras

These cameras will take good-quality pictures of almost any subject, in most types of lighting. Some models give you a choice of two different lenses to use – a wide-angle lens for broad scenes or a telephoto lens for close-up pictures. Other models have a zoom lens, which starts off as wide-angle but, as you press a button, zooms into a telephoto.

● *Autofocus*

● *Good autoexposure*

● *Built-in flash*

● *Automatic film transport*

Zoom control button

Autofocus light receptor

Viewfinder

Built-in flash/red eye reduction lamp

Shutter-release button

Autofocus light projector

Lens

Metering window

Self-timer/remote control lamp

Viewfinder (behind)

Hot shoe

On/off switch

LCD panel

Camera strap eyelet

Focusing ring

Self-timer indicator

Shutter-release button

Aperture control ring

Lens

35 mm single lens reflex (SLR) cameras

SLR cameras are extremely versatile because you can take the lens off the camera body and fit a different one. This means that with the right accessories you can tackle almost any kind of photography. Also, the scene through the viewfinder is always accurate. SLRs range from simple to very sophisticated models, and can be manually operated, fully automatic, or both. You can also attach a separate flash gun, which gives better lighting than built-in flash.

● *Add-on flash gun*

● *Choice of autofocus, manual focus or both*

● *Choice of different types of autoexposure*

● *Automatic film transport*

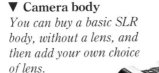

35 mm SLR system lenses and accessories

The range of lenses and accessories for 35 mm SLRs is vast. Most camera manufacturers have a system of lenses that fit the models they make, and these include lenses so wide that they see behind the camera, and telephotos so powerful that they can fill the frame with a picture of the moon.

Accessories include microscope adaptors to take pictures of objects smaller than the eye can see and waterproof cases for underwater pictures of fish and coral.

▼ Camera body
You can buy a basic SLR body, without a lens, and then add your own choice of lens.

Nikon F-601M

Lens-release button

Lens mount

► Telephoto zoom lens
This comes in various focal lengths. It allows you to zoom-in and take different-sized pictures of your subject from the same camera position, by increasing the size of your image in the frame.

► Wide-angle to short telephoto zoom lens
This versatile lens allows you to photograph broad scenes, as well as moderately close-up, detailed shots, without changing camera position.

35–70mm

Plunger

Attachment screw

▲ Portrait lens
A focal length of about 85–90 mm is considered to be ideal for taking portraits since this will allow you to get close enough to crop out unimportant background detail, without distorting facial features.

▲ Cable release
This is an extension cable that allows you to release the shutter without touching the camera. You use a cable release, usually for a slow shutter speed, when it is important that you don't jar the camera.

Adjustable flash head

Canon

Flash gun slides into hot shoe

◄ Flash
You can attach a separate flash unit to all SLRs by sliding it into a special fitting on top of the camera called a 'hot shoe'. Some SLRs also have a built-in flash.

UV filter

Polarizing filter

▲ Filters
Filters are coloured discs that fit over the camera lens. They alter the way that light affects the film to enhance colour or create special effects.

Canon EOS-1

Built-in flash

Lens

Close-up lever

Shutter-release button (on side)

Lighten/darken control

Picture exit slot

Viewfinder

Instant-picture Polaroid cameras

Polaroid cameras are unlike any others because the film starts to develop as soon as you take the picture and is completely finished in about one minute. Although the pictures are instant they are expensive per shot and the quality can be variable. The cameras range from very basic models to ones with automatic features.

- *Autofocus*
- *Built-in flash*
- *Autoexposure*

Still video camera

The newest type of camera doesn't use film at all. Instead it uses a floppy disk, much like the types used in computers, to store your pictures. Prints can be made from the disk, but the camera is designed to show your pictures on an ordinary television set. It uses the same principles as a video camera, only the pictures are still. Once your pictures are on screen, you can record them on your VCR and then reuse the disk for new pictures.

- *Fixed focus*
- *Autoexposure*
- *Built-in flash*

Shutter-release/ play button

LCD display panel

Viewfinder

Flash on/off button

Erase button

Date entry button

Lens

Self-timer indicator

Video signal output terminal

Built-in flash

Floppy disk

PROFESSIONAL CAMERAS

Professional photographers usually use large-format cameras when they are taking pictures in a studio. This is because the film they use is also large format, so the negatives are much bigger and pick up very fine detail, giving better quality images. The lighting is controlled using special electronic flash lighting systems that can be finely balanced to give the exact amount of light needed.

WHICH FILM?

FILM comes in a variety of different types and sizes. The size of film that you will need to buy depends on the camera you have, but there are different types of film to choose between for most cameras. The type that you choose will depend partly on how you want your pictures to appear when they have been developed.

The most popular type of film is colour negative, from which colour prints are made. Black-and-white negative film is also available and gives black-and-white prints. If you want your pictures to be developed into slides for use in a projector, you will need to buy transparency, or slide, film.

Each type of film also comes in different speeds. You can tell the speed of a film by the ISO (International Standards Organization) number on the packet. If you are going to be taking pictures in dull light you will need a fast film such as ISO 400 or more. For bright light conditions, choose a slower film such as ISO 100 or 200.

▲ **Instant picture Polaroid film**
Film for instant picture or Polaroid cameras comes in packs of individual sheets which are self-developing.

▼ **Size of film**
35 mm film is used for compacts and SLRs. 110 cameras and Polaroids use their own special films. You can buy larger format and sheet film, for professional cameras.

110 film cartridge

35 mm film cassette

◄ **Colour negative and print**
After processing, your colour negative looks like this, with all the colours of the original scene reversed. In fact, all the information is reversed, and this is why it is called a negative. The negative is reversed again to produce a print.

FILM SPEED

The 'speed' of a film refers to how sensitive it is to light. Faster films are coated with larger, lumpier grains of silver salts, which require less light to react. So you should use a fast film when the lighting conditions for your photographs are poor, such as in dull weather. The higher the ISO number on the carton, the faster the film is, and the more sensitive it is to light. For really poor light, you can even buy ISO 1600 or 3200, but you will find that pictures taken with very fast films tend to look quite grainy.

◄ Coarse or fine?
Slow, fine-grain ISO 100 film (far left) records even small detail. Fast ISO 1000 film (left) gives a more grainy image.

ISO 100 film   ISO 1000 film

▲ Colour negative 110 film and print
Used only in 110 cameras, the negative is small. Prints need to be enlarged a great deal and so quality can be poor.

▲ Black-and-white negative and print
A black-and-white negative has dark tones where the scene was bright, and light tones where it was dark. When the print is made, tones are reversed again, showing light and dark areas correctly.

Card mount

▲ Slide film
When you look at transparency or slide film, the scene looks just as it did when you took the picture. This is so that the pictures can be projected on to a screen or wall.

Plastic mount

◄ Colour slides
The film processor cuts your film strip up into individual frames and mounts each one in a cardboard or plastic holder ready for projection.

USING YOUR CAMERA

WHATEVER kind of camera you have, even if it's automatic, there are some simple basics you need to learn and understand, so that you can use the camera effectively. One rule you should learn from the start is always to squeeze the camera's shutter-release button gently – never jab it, as this will give you shaky pictures. These pages contain information to get you started, but don't forget that you can also refer to your camera manual.

LOOK IT UP!

Aperture p 13
Shutter p 13
Depth of field p 43, 88

Holding your camera

◀ Keep your balance
Choose a well-balanced position, with your elbows comfortably tucked into your body, so that you can hold the camera really steady.

▲ Check your view
Keep your fingers folded away from the lens. Check that the camera strap is also tucked well back before you take a picture.

Picture frame marks

Viewfinder

Parallax marks

View seen through viewfinder

View recorded by lens

▲ Using a support
If you need extra support for your camera, particularly when using a slow shutter speed, rest your camera against a solid object such as a tree or gate.

Using a compact camera
You must keep your subject within the corner marks of your viewfinder. But, because the viewfinder is above and to one side of the lens, there is a slight difference between what you see and what the lens sees. This is called parallax error, and it can result in your chopping off part of a close-up subject. To avoid this, make sure the important parts of your picture are within the extra parallax marks.

The SLR viewfinder

An SLR viewfinder has a central focusing aid, such as this split-ring. When the two halves of the circle are aligned, the image is correctly focused. A band around the split-ring, called a microprism collar, shimmers until the subject is in focus. A display in the viewfinder frame will indicate the shutter speed and aperture size that the camera's autoexposure has selected.

SLR viewfinder

Microprism collar

Split-ring focusing aid

Recommended shutter speed

Recommended aperture size

Shutter speed

The shutter speed helps to determine the amount of exposure the film receives. The speeds are marked in fractions of a second. Setting a shutter speed of $^1/_{125}$, for example, means that the shutter opens and allows light to reach the film for $^1/_{125}$ of a second. Each time you increase the shutter speed, you double the length of time the shutter remains open. The shutter also determines the precise moment that you take the picture.

Small aperture

'F stops'
Aperture control ring

f22 is a very small aperture. The blades are almost closed and allow only a little light through to the film.

Large aperture

'F stops'
Aperture control ring

f2.8 is a wide aperture. The blades open to allow lots of light through.

Lens aperture

The lens aperture works together with the shutter speed to determine the amount of light reaching the film. Aperture sizes are referred to as 'f stops', and the larger the number of the 'f stop', the smaller the size of the aperture. On most lenses, the apertures are f2, f2.8, f4, f5.6, f8, f11, f16, and f22, with f2 the largest size and f22 the smallest. Each time you move up the scale, you double the size of the aperture, and so double the amount of light reaching the film. By balancing the size of the aperture with the shutter speed, you will select the right exposure. This will probably be done automatically by your camera, but sometimes you may wish to change the exposure manually. The numbers in the viewfinder display will blink or glow to indicate when you have selected the correct aperture to go with the shutter speed you are using.

HOW APERTURE SIZE AFFECTS FOCUS

As well as controlling film exposure, by letting more or less light into the camera, the size of the lens aperture also has an effect on the amount of the picture that is sharply focused. No matter where you focus the lens directly, there is always an area of your picture, both in front of and behind this point, which is also sharply focused. This band of focus is known as the depth of field. As you make the aperture size larger, the depth of field decreases, or becomes shallower.

Small aperture
A small aperture increases the depth of field, increasing the area around the subject that is sharply focused. If it is important that all the subject elements in your picture are sharp, use a slower shutter speed so that you can select a small lens aperture.

Large aperture
When the aperture is large, your subject will be the only sharp element in the picture. The depth of field will be very shallow. To create this effect, use the manual controls to select a large aperture. Use a faster shutter speed to correct the exposure.

COMPOSING YOUR PICTURES

Good photographs are not created just by being able to use your camera – the most important skill is making an interesting choice and arrangement of objects within your picture area. This arrangement is called composition.

When you look through the viewfinder, think about what you want the focus of your picture to be. Will it be in the foreground or background of the picture? Look at your subject from different angles and spend time choosing your viewpoint. Consider the shapes, lines, and colours that you can see and look for something that will give your picture impact. By moving your camera position you may, for example, be able to include a brightly coloured flower in an otherwise completely green field, or show the subject framed by trees.

You can pick up lots of tips from other people's pictures – in books, magazines, and newspapers. Keep a scrapbook of photographs that work well and use them for reference later.

▼ Leafy landscape
The smaller pictures (below) show less successful views of this landscape, tried out by the photographer before he took the picture on the right. They do not have an obvious main subject to tie the composition together.

▼ City scene
The picture below right is the most successful of these three cityscapes. By including the ship in the foreground, the photographer has given the city scene depth and scale.

22

▲ **Unusual viewpoint**
Even everyday things such as trees can make an interesting composition if you find an unusual viewpoint for your picture. This photographer lay on the ground on his back with the camera pointing directly upwards.

▲
Here the photographer has included the windmill as a point of focus. The strong lines of the path lead the viewer's eye to this point.

▲ **Rural reflections**
This striking landscape picture was made even better by balancing the mountains and hillsides with their mirror image, created in the calm waters of the lake.

◀ **Concentric circles**
These fungi, taken in close-up using a macro lens, are a good example of the interesting compositions you can create by emphasizing natural pattern and texture.

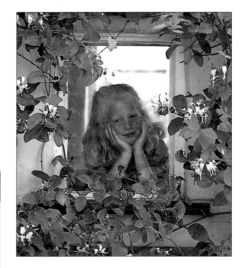

LOOK IT UP!
Natural light p 24 - 25
Landscapes and Cityscapes p 60 - 63
Macro lens p 90

▲ **Frames within frames**
This picture has many layers. The outer frame is created by the photograph edges, the second by the honeysuckle, and the third by the window frame.

NATURAL LIGHT

MOST photographs are taken using natural light. Because this light comes from the sun, it is constantly changing. The quality of light changes with the seasons, with the weather, and the time of day. All these variations of light will affect the appearance of your photographs and the exposure needed for your film.

Most cameras automatically select the correct exposure, although many SLRs can also be operated manually. The speed of film you choose will also help to compensate for dull or very bright light. But you can use these varying types and angles of light to create different effects and atmospheres in your photographs.

▲ **Early morning**
As the sun rises in the sky, its low angle produces long shadows that give an image depth and texture. As the land is cold, the air can be very cool and clear, and this will give your picture a sharp quality.

Winter

Spring

Seasonal light

The landscape changes with the seasons, from spring when the trees burst into leaf, to winter when they become bare skeletons of branches. But it also looks different because the sun's light changes as the seasons change. In summer, the sun is high in the sky and very intense. In winter, it barely climbs above the horizon, so it is far weaker. The light from a low sun has to travel through a great volume of atmosphere, so it is scattered. This creates a much softer lighting effect.

Summer

▲▶ **Seasonal sights**
These pictures show how a landscape can change dramatically as the seasons pass.

Autumn

▲ Midday

At midday, light floods the landscape and its intensity can rob the scene of colour and definition. As the sun moves overhead, shadows become short and very dense, increasing contrast dramatically.

▲ Evening

As the sun goes down in the evening, the light changes once again, giving a much softer appearance to the landscape. The low sun, directly behind the cactus, has produced a near-silhouette that looks very dramatic.

▲ Snowy scene

Snow and frost will often give your pictures a blue tinge because they reflect the ultraviolet parts of light.

◀ Foggy weather

Fog and mist are more likely in early morning. They cling to landscapes, giving the light a hazy quality.

▲ Rainy weather

As this picture shows, rain can create a soft lighting effect, which can give your photograph atmosphere.

25

FLASH LIGHT

YOU will need to use flash, or artificial light, in situations where there is not enough natural light reaching the film to expose it properly. Flash is almost always needed for indoor photography where the light is very limited. It is used out of doors in dull or evening light. Flash can be used in very bright light to reduce the contrast between light and dark areas of a picture. If you take a picture with the sun directly behind your subject (called backlighting), you can use flash to fill in the areas facing the camera that are in shadow.

Most cameras have a built-in automatic flash that runs off batteries. SLRs, as well as sometimes having a built-in flash, have a special connector on top of the camera called a 'hot shoe'. This is where you attach an add-on flash gun.

When to use flash

Flash is ideal to use when there is not enough daylight in a scene indoors or outdoors. The colour of the flash light is balanced for most colour films, so the results will look natural.

▼ In the dark
If the subject is too far away from the flash when it fires, the scene will look unnaturally dark.

▲ Get it right
The flash must be the correct distance away from the subject to achieve the correct lighting results.

► Too close
If the flash is too close, the subject will appear bleached of colour.

Direct flash

Flash (either built in or an add-on accessory gun) pointed directly at the subject produces a stark, almost clinical type of lighting that can be quite unflattering. All of the subtle gradations of colour or tone will be missing, and areas will be either lit or unlit.

Diffused flash

Placing diffusing material (material that scatters light) such as tissue paper over the flash will soften the lighting effect and give a more flattering result. The distinction between lit and unlit areas becomes less obvious.

Bounced flash

If you use an SLR with an add-on flash gun, you can angle the flash head so that the light bounces off the ceiling or wall before reaching your subject. As the light is not direct, it is much softer.

Fill-in flash

Even when lighting levels are generally high enough to take a picture by natural light alone, there may still be occasions when you need to use flash. If the subject is backlit (left), for example, the side of the subject facing the camera will be very dark. To overcome this, you can direct flash just into the shadow areas to brighten them a little (far left). This is known as fill-in flash.

DEVELOPING YOUR FILM

I F you have access to a darkroom, perhaps at
school, you could try to develop your own
black-and-white film to make negatives for
printing. The technique described here is suitable
for 35 mm black-and-white film only. Although
the chemicals used in film developing are not very
dangerous, you must always take care not to
splash any of the concentrated chemicals on to
your skin or into your eyes, especially since
some of the time you will be working in total
darkness. You may need an adult to help you.

How film is constructed

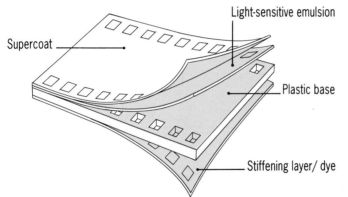

A piece of film is constructed of many fine layers. The top
layer of gelatine, known as a supercoat, protects the layers
beneath. Under this is the important layer of light-sensitive
emulsion, made up of millions of minute grains of silver-
halide crystals. The thickest layer is the plastic base of
the film, but there is also a stiffening layer to prevent the film
curling, as well as a layer of dye to prevent light reflecting
back up through the emulsion from the film base.

Equipment

Darkroom layout

*The illustration below shows where the equipment in a well-
organized darkroom should be positioned. For safety, the
darkroom is divided into wet and dry areas.*

Dry area
All 'dry' processes are
carried out on this side of
the room.

Wet area
All 'wet' processes are
carried out on this
side of the room.

Developing tank This can be made
of plastic or stainless steel. Once the lid
is in place, the chemicals can be poured
in but no light can enter.

Chemicals The three
chemicals you need are
developer, stop bath, and
fixer. The developer
produces the negative; the
stop bath halts the action
of the developer; and the
fixer dissolves unwanted
silver crystals and makes
the film insensitive to light.

Step-by-step developing

1 Arrange the developing tank and other equipment so you can find them in the dark. Turn out the light and open the top of the film cassette. Slide the film spool out and cut off the shaped end of the film strip. Cut between sprocket holes to leave a clean edge.

2 Load the film on to the spiral by threading it under the teeth, and rotate the sides back and forth to wind it on. When you reach the end of the film, cut off the cassette reel. Wind the last few centimetres in and tuck the last bit of film into the spiral.

3 Put the loaded spiral into the developing tank, fitting it over the centre core. Put the lid on, securing it tightly. Now you can turn on the lights. Mix up the developing liquid according to the manufacturer's instructions on the container.

4 Remove the cap from the centre of the lid and pour the developer in. Start the timer immediately and put the cap back in place. Rap the tank smartly on the edge of a hard surface to dislodge any air bubbles clinging to the film.

5 You must agitate the tank for 15 seconds during every minute of development, by constantly turning it upside down. After development, pour out the developer and pour in the stop bath. Agitate the tank for 30 seconds.

6 Pour the stop bath out and refill with fixer for the recommended time. The chemicals can all be reused a number of times. Pour them carefully into storage containers and note how many films they have been used to process.

7 After removing the fixer, the film is developed and is insensitive to light. To remove all traces of chemical residue, take the lid off the tank and place the tank and spiral under *gently* running water for at least 30 minutes. Too much water pressure may damage the still soft emulsion.

8 Wetting agent, added at the final washing stage, stops water droplets clinging to the film and leaving marks. Carefully unwind the film from the spiral and wipe it once with a perfectly clean pair of squeegee tongs. Attach a film clip to one end of the film and hang it up to dry in a dust-free area.

THE FINISHED NEGATIVE

Black-and-white negatives have dark tones where the scene was light, and light tones where the scene was dark. All the information is reversed, which is why they are called negatives.

Dark tones

Light tones

Making a Print

Using the negatives, you can make prints of your pictures. You will need to do this in a darkroom because the printing paper is also sensitive to most types of light. However, with black-and-white printing paper, you can work with a special red-coloured 'safelight' on at all times. But you must use only the recommended low-wattage lightbulb.

How a print is produced

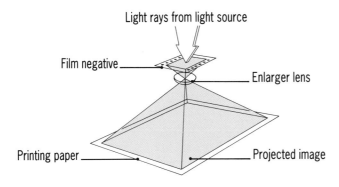

Light rays from light source

Film negative

Enlarger lens

Printing paper

Projected image

Only the clear areas of the film let light from the enlarger (right) through to the printing paper. Where the negative is black, the light is blocked; where it is grey, only some light can get through. The parts of the paper that receive light turn black, or a shade of grey, when developed. Areas that don't receive light remain white.

Because the tones of the subject were reversed as a negative and reversed again when printed, the finished print shows the original tones of the composition restored.

Equipment

Measuring cylinder

Plastic developing trays

Print tongs

Developing chemicals

Thermometer

Timer

Column

Elevation knob

Focusing knob

Negative holder

Focusing bellows

Red filter

Enlarging lens

Timer

Printing easel

Baseboard

The head of an enlarger has a built-in light and a lens. Between the light and lens is a film carrier to hold negatives in position. Light travels through the film and into the lens. This can be focused until a sharp image appears on the baseboard below. The lens also has an aperture control to make the light brighter or dimmer for different negatives. The exposure time is controlled by turning the enlarger light on and off. A red filter swings over the lens to stop the light affecting the paper while you are focusing the image.

Photographic paper This comes in a variety of grades and surfaces. For your first attempts at printing, try grade 2 paper which is quick to process and dry.

Chemicals You will need developer to produce the image on the paper, stop bath to halt the developing process, and fixer to fix the image and stop any further chemical reaction.

Step-by-step printing

1 Cut the film into strips of six negatives. Place a negative into the film holder of the enlarger with the dull side facing down. Mix up the chemicals using the manufacturer's instructions, and pour them into separate dishes.

2 Turn the room lights out and the safelight and enlarger on. Adjust the height of the head until the image on the baseboard fits inside the arms of the printing easel, which should be set to the size of paper you are using.

3 Focus the image using the focusing control on the lens. Set the aperture to the largest size, as this will give you the brightest image. Use a magnifier to check the focus of your image, and to make sure the negative is not distorted.

4 Swing the red filter over the lens. Position a piece of printing paper, shiny side up, in the printing easel. Check the focus, turn the enlarger off, and remove the red filter. Reduce the aperture by two stops to give a sharper result.

5 Make a test strip. Cover up three-quarters of the paper with card. Turn the enlarger on and give a 10-second exposure. Move the card to expose another strip for a further 10 seconds. Continue until all the paper is exposed.

6 Slip the test strip carefully into the tray of developer. Rock the tray gently to make sure the solution reaches all of the paper's surface. Leave for the time recommended by the manufacturer's instructions on the container.

7 Use print tongs to remove the paper from the developer (allow excess developer to drain off) and place it in the stop bath. Agitate the stop bath for the recommended time. Using the other pair of print tongs, place the print into the dish of fixer.

8 After about 1 minute, remove the test strip print and wash it under running water. It will show strips of different exposure times. Decide which exposure is best (it may be between two strips – say, 25 seconds). Expose and develop a fresh sheet of paper to make your print.

9 Finished prints should be washed in clean running water for at least 30 minutes. This will remove all traces of chemicals. Finally, dry your prints. There are two types of printing paper – hang resin-coated paper prints up to dry, but dry fibre-based paper prints flat.

FAULT FINDER

Badly-framed subject – parallax marks ignored

Framing errors

Correct framing within parallax marks

E VEN professional photographers with many years of experience make mistakes from time to time. This is always disappointing, especially if you can't easily take the picture again, but mistakes can be useful if you learn from them. Then you can avoid making the same mistakes in the future. This section of the book identifies many common errors, and explains how you can correct them.

What went wrong?
A compact camera was used too close to the subject and you ignored the viewfinder framing lines, or parallax marks.

What can I do?
Framing errors occur because compact cameras have a viewfinder separate from the lens. Make sure that you keep within the framing marks, and within the parallax marks for close-ups.

Camera shake

Blurred image

Lens obstruction

Finger intrudes into picture

What went wrong?
The camera moved while you were taking the picture.

What can I do?
Always stand in a comfortable and balanced way, so you can keep the camera really steady. If possible, use a faster shutter speed (such as $\frac{1}{125}$ second), which makes camera shake less likely. Faster shutter speeds are also important with telephoto lenses. Because they are heavy, they show up even slight camera movement. If you have to use a slower speed, support the camera on a firm, even surface, and always press the shutter-release button gently.

What went wrong?
A finger, or part of the camera strap, was in front of the lens as the picture was taken.

What can I do?
This usually only happens with a compact camera because of its separate viewfinder. Before taking each picture make sure that your fingers, hair, camera strap, and any other possible obstructions are well away from the lens.

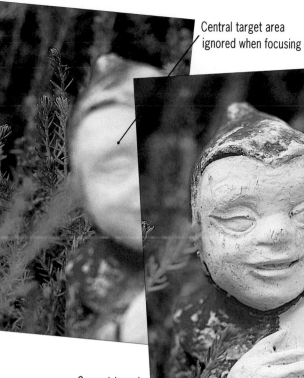

Central target area
ignored when focusing

Correct target
area for focusing

Focusing errors

What went wrong?
With an automatic camera, the subject was probably not in the central target area, used by the autofocus system to focus the camera. On a manual camera, you did not set the focusing controls on the lens accurately.

What can I do?
With an automatic camera, pay attention to where the subject is located in the viewfinder. On a manual, check the focusing screen carefully before shooting.

Vignettes

Dark area
around image

What went wrong?
The edge of the picture has been obscured. There appears to be a dark area, or vignette, surrounding part of the image.

What can I do?
This only occurs on SLRs. The most likely cause is that a lens hood, designed for a standard or telephoto lens, was used on a wide-angle lens, or zoom set to wide-angle. Sometimes a vignette is also caused when a polarizing filter is fitted to the lens, as this has a double-depth rim.

Lens flare

Overexposed
area
caused by
flare from sun

What went wrong?
The picture was taken with the lens pointing directly at the sun.

Flare corrected

What can I do?
Change camera position so that the sun is masked behind an object, such as a tree, and not shining directly into the lens. This should eliminate the flare while keeping the same lighting effect on the subject.

- Camera shake
- Framing errors
- Lens obstruction
- Vignettes
- Lens flare
- Focusing errors

Tram lines

 Tram line

What went wrong?
The film surface is very delicate and it has been scratched, probably by grit inside the camera.

What can I do?
Make sure that the inside of your camera is completely clean, particularly the film pressure plate on the inside of the camera back. Nothing can be done to correct scratches after they have occurred.

Overlapping frames

Overlapping double image

What went wrong?
The most likely cause is that the film was not properly loaded and so has not wound on after each picture was taken.

What can I do?
Follow the instructions in your camera manual for loading film. Usually the camera has a system that allows you to check that film is winding on properly. You will also find this in the manual.

Flash exposure problems

Correct

Too light – highlights bleached

What went wrong?
The flash was either too close or too far from the subject when fired.

What can I do?
Make sure you are the correct distance from your subject (check your manual for distances). Flash light reduces in intensity as it travels. This limits you to taking pictures within about 3 m (10 ft) of your subject. This isn't a problem indoors, but outdoor subject distances are often greater. Get closer to your subject or use a faster film. Overexposed flash pictures are caused by being too close or by using an aperture that is too wide. Read the flash manual to find the correct aperture for each subject distance.

Too dark – background detail dense

Fogging

What went wrong
Until film is fully processed it remains sensitive to light. Any stray light reaching the film will make the image 'misty'.

What can I do?
This orange 'veil' is typical of film that has been exposed to light other than that from the lens. Make sure that you load a new film away from bright light, and that you rewind the film completely into its cassette before removing it from the camera. You cannot correct this problem after it has occurred.

Orange 'veil'

Flash synchronization

Shutter blind obscures image

What went wrong?
This problem is confined to SLRs and is caused when the flash fires before the shutter is fully open.

What can I do?
With an SLR, you must set the shutter to the correct speed for flash synchronization – usually $^1/_{125}$ second – or to the lightning flash symbol. Check your user's manual. If you have done this and the problem persists, the camera will need to be taken in for repair.

Red eye

Red spots in eyes

What went wrong?
Because the flash is close to the camera lens, the light has reflected back from the blood vessels in the subject's eyes.

What can I do?
This problem is most common on compact cameras, although many now are fitted with an anti-red eye flash facility. If you can't use an add-on flash or bounce the light, as with an SLR, ask the subject to glance away from the camera as you take the picture.

Processing errors

Correct colour balance

Too much blue

Too much yellow

What went wrong?
Colour errors affecting all of the prints, such as those shown here, are likely to have been caused during processing.

What can I do?
If the negatives are not affected, take bad prints back to the processor (with the negatives) and ask for a free reprint.

- Tram lines
- Fogging
- Overlapping frames
- Flash exposure problems
- Red eye
- Flash synchronization
- Processing errors

LOOKING AND LEARNING

Now that you have learnt how your camera works and how to use it, it's time to go out and take some pictures. This part of the book is divided into projects, each one covering a different subject area. The projects are designed to show you the wide range of picture opportunities available, as well as different techniques you can use to create unusual compositions and special effects. You will learn how to take portraits of people and photograph animals and nature. Landscapes, cityscapes and buildings provide plenty of scope to practise your photographic skills. Techniques for capturing movement are covered on the sport and action pages. There is information on lenses and set-ups needed for still life and close-up photography. You can also learn how to play around with images to make abstract designs, montages and panoramas, and create unusual lighting effects.

PEOPLE PORTRAITS

MOST people buy their first camera to take pictures of family and friends, so a portrait will probably be one of the first photographs you take. Before you take the picture, think about the type of image you want. You can ask people to pose for you, but some of the best pictures happen when the subject doesn't know that a picture is being taken. This type of informal picture is called a candid photograph. For posed portraits, it is a good idea to take lots of pictures to help your subject overcome any shyness.

Choose your background and camera angle carefully and decide what will be best for the type of shot you want. If you are using a camera with a wide-angle lens, such as a simple compact, remember that moving in very close may distort your subject's features. A zoom lens of about 90 mm is excellent for portraits.

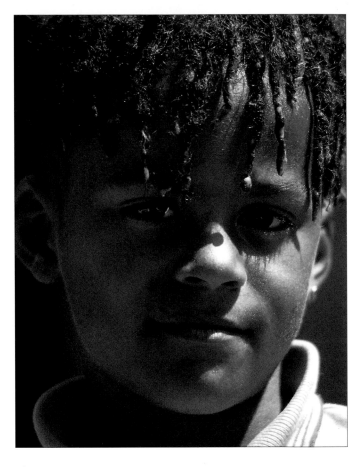

▲ **Posed portrait**
Portraits are usually thought of as formal, posed pictures, such as this photograph.

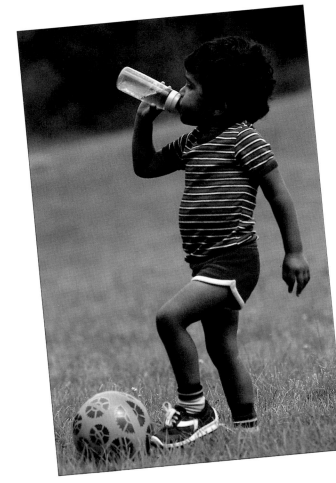

◄ **Simple shots**
Simple, candid shots are very effective and can be taken easily with a telephoto lens or zoom. This allows you to stand well back, so the subject is not likely to notice the camera.

LOOK IT UP!
SLR lenses p 16, 90, 91
Parallax error p 20
Self-portraits p 80–81

◄ **Tips on candids**
If you don't want your subject to know you are taking a picture, you will have to blend into the background as much as possible. Use a zoom lens, and preset the focus and exposure controls so that you will be ready to shoot when your subject is naturally distracted. You may need to support the camera if you are using a heavy lens.

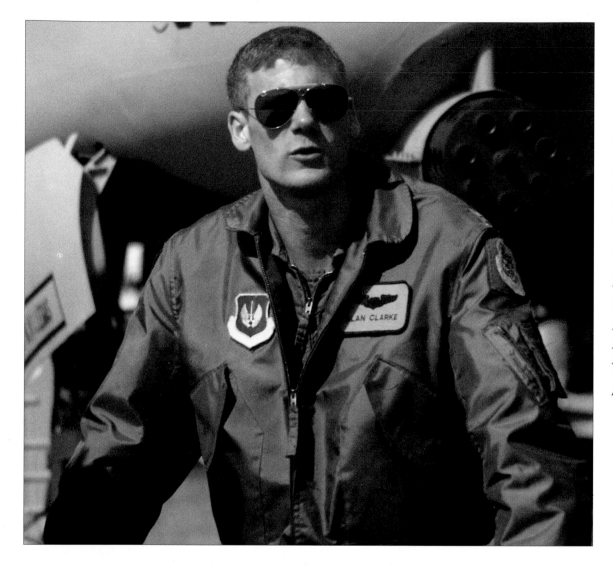

◀ ▼ **Using longer lenses**
Telephoto or zoom lenses allow you to close in and capture facial expressions when you are taking candid shots, such as the collection on this page. All of the subjects were engrossed in what they were doing and totally unaware of the photographer. Shots such as these often tell a lot more about the person being photographed than posed pictures.

The subject is positioned so that her face is lit by direct window light. However, as the light is only coming from one direction, one side of her face is in shadow.

The picture above shows a well balanced, naturally-lit facial portrait. You can take a formal portrait quite easily using the light coming in through a window. The pictures on the right show how, by reflecting or diffusing the light, you can create different effects and atmospheres in your pictures.

Using daylight film indoors

The photographer has added a secondary light source, directed at the right side of the face, to soften the shadowed area. But the effect is still quite harsh.

Using normal daylight-balanced film with indoor electric lighting will give your pictures a warm, orange cast. This can be quite a flattering lighting effect.

By covering the window with white mesh or cloth, the light is diffused, or scattered. This gives a softer and more flattering lighting effect. By adding a reflector, the shadows are further softened.

▼ ▶ Group portraits

The more people there are in a picture, the more difficult it is to arrange them so they can all be seen. Choose the background carefully, then organise the group so that the tallest are at the back and smallest in the front. This is particularly important for a formal group shot (below), but even in a simple group line-up (right), you still need to be able to see all the faces.

LOOK IT UP!

Flash light
p 26 – 27

Natural light
p 24 – 25

Daylight-balanced
film p 88

▼ Family faces

This family group is a much more relaxed shot. Although the subjects have not been formally arranged, they are posing directly for the camera.

ANIMAL PORTRAITS

Good animal photographs can be quite tricky to take. You cannot direct animals to pose for you as people do, so you need lots of patience.

The easiest animal subject to use is a pet and it is best to photograph your pet outside, as flash might frighten it. For an active type of animal, such as a dog, you could try taking some action photographs. Think carefully about how you compose your pictures and experiment with unusual viewpoints and camera angles. You could even get in close for a dramatic view that perhaps does not show all of the subject.

Take a trip to a zoo or wildlife park for pictures of more unusual animals. If you telephone beforehand you may be able to find out the feeding times and take some really exciting shots!

GETTING THE EYELINE RIGHT

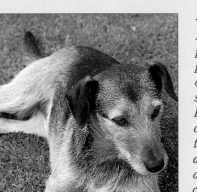

◄ From above
Many people take pictures of their pets looking down on them from a standing position. But, because the camera is above the eyeline of the animal, it is difficult to capture its character.

◄ At eye-level
This picture was taken with the camera at the same level as the dog's eyes. By looking directly into the animal's face, the picture communicates much more of the dog's individuality.

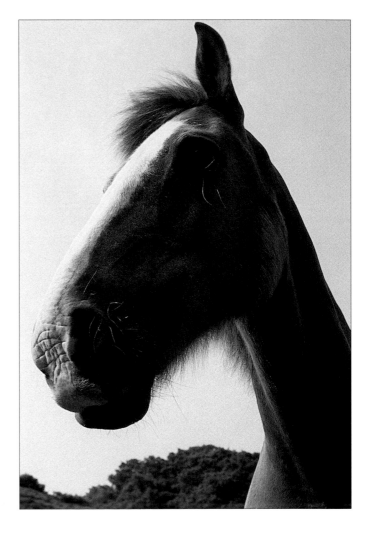

▲ Dramatic angle
For this portrait, the photographer used a wide-angle lens, moved in close, and took the picture from below.

LOOK IT UP!
SLR lenses p 16, 90, 91
Depth of field p 21, 88

◄ Filling the frame
This photograph of a peacock was taken in a wildlife park. The bird was used to visitors and very tame, so allowed the photographer to get close enough to fill the viewfinder.

▲ Feeding animals
You can use a small amount of food to encourage your subject to come in closer to the camera, like this squirrel. But never feed caged animals at a zoo.

▲ ► Coping with wire cages
If you take pictures at a zoo, it can be difficult to avoid the wire fences that often surround the enclosures (above). If you have an SLR camera with a telephoto lens or zoom, you can get around this problem. Stand as close to the wire as possible and select your widest lens aperture (most cameras will then automatically correct the exposure). As you focus, you will see in the viewfinder that the wire seems almost to disappear. This is because of the shallow depth of field of wide apertures on telephoto lenses. Although the subject will be in focus, the background will not be, and the wire will be so out of focus it becomes almost transparent (right).

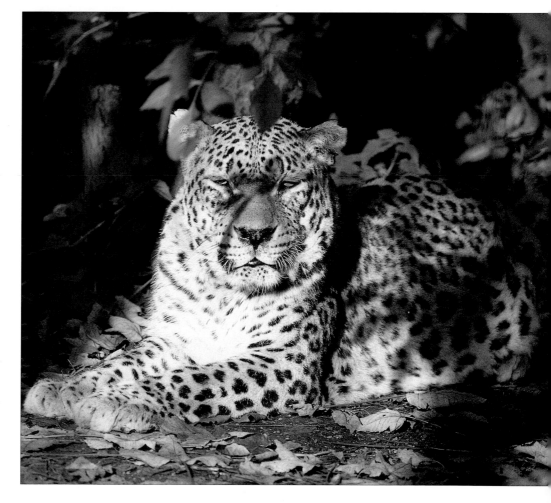

SPORT AND ACTION

THERE are two ways you can give your pictures a real sense of movement – that is either by 'freezing' or 'blurring' the action. For both of these you will need to be able to alter the shutter speed on your camera. On an SLR, you do this by moving the shutter speed dial. The aperture size will then need to be changed to give the correct exposure. Most compact cameras do not allow you to change the shutter speed manually, but by altering the speed of film, you can often get the autoexposure to select a fast or slow shutter speed.

To freeze action, select a fast shutter speed. This means that the shutter will only open for the briefest instant, so won't record the subject moving. With an automatic camera, take pictures in bright light and on fast film, and the autoexposure will select a fast shutter speed.

To create 'blur', use a slow shutter speed so the subject moves while the shutter is open. With an automatic camera, shoot in poor light on slow film, and the autoexposure should then select a slow shutter speed.

Other techniques include 'panning' the camera and using flash. If flash is your main source of light, such as at night, it will freeze movement because the burst of light lasts for only a fraction of a second.

▲ Mixed techniques
This exciting action picture is the result of mixing flash with a slow shutter speed and exaggerated camera movement.

▲ Slow shutter speed
If you choose a slow shutter speed, such as 1/15 second, with a moving subject you will get a 'blurred' effect. But remember that with a slow shutter speed you need to support the camera to keep it perfectly still.

◄ Fast shutter speed
For this picture the photographer used a shutter speed of 1/500 second, which was fast enough to freeze even the fastest-moving part of the subject – the bicycle wheels.

► Flash and daylight
Using flash in daylight means that you will increase the contrast between the subject, which will appear very bright, and the background, which will appear much darker.

Capturing movement

Position 1

Position 2

Position 3

Position 1

Position 2

Position 3

Direction of camera swing

▲ Pivoting the camera

The diagram (above) shows how the pictures on the right were taken. Using a fast shutter speed, the photographer changed the position of the camera by pivoting it to line up with the subject at three separate points. Although the photographer has captured the moving subject, there is very little feeling of action in the image. Compare this with the panned photograph (below), which has a greater sense of movement.

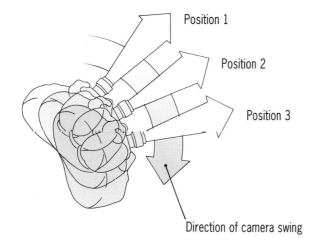

◄ Action panning

Panning means swinging the camera in an arc to keep up with a moving subject. For this to be effective, you need to select a shutter speed suitable for the speed of your subject. For example, with a running figure a shutter speed of about 1/30 second should 'blur' the still parts of your picture, while giving you a sharp image of the subject. With this racing car, you would have to pan the camera much faster and so a shutter speed of 1/250 second is more appropriate. The background will still 'blur' because the camera is moving a lot faster to keep up with the subject.

▲ ▶ Canoe views

These two pictures, both of canoeists in action, show how important it is to think carefully about the viewpoint you choose. Action pictures are often more exciting if the subject is large in the frame. Get as close as you can to the action or use a telephoto or zoom lens.

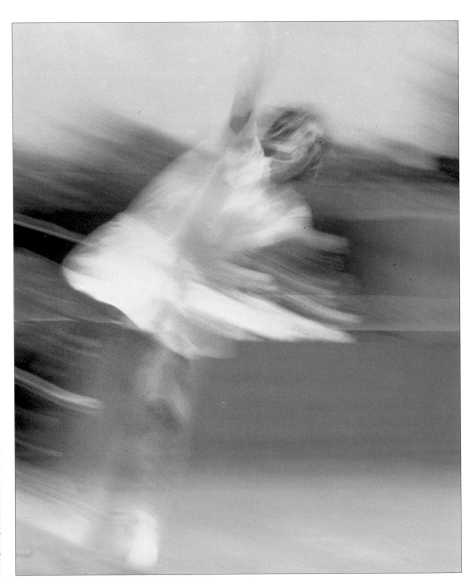

▲ ▶ Changing views

If your camera allows you to alter the shutter speed, you can photograph the same subject in different ways. Choose a fast speed for 'frozen' action pictures (above) or a slow speed for more atmospheric pictures (right).

LOOK IT UP!

Shutter speed p 21, 90
Autoexposure p 14, 88
Aperture p 13, 21, 88
Flash p 16, 26 - 27
Composition p 22 - 23
Film speed p 18,19

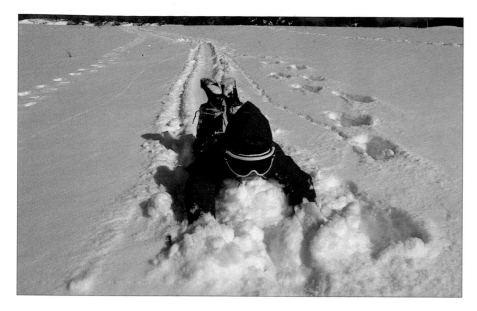

◄ **Toboggan tracks**
This picture is simple but effective because the photographer has used a low viewpoint to emphasize the pile of snow in front of the tobogganist, and the tracks made as he travelled down the slope.

▼ **Speeding skateboarder**
Although the background is blurred, the skateboarder is frozen because he is lit mainly by the burst of light from a flash.

▼ ► **Peak of action**
This is a perfect moment to capture on film. The skateboarders are balanced at the peak of action, ready to hurtle downwards.

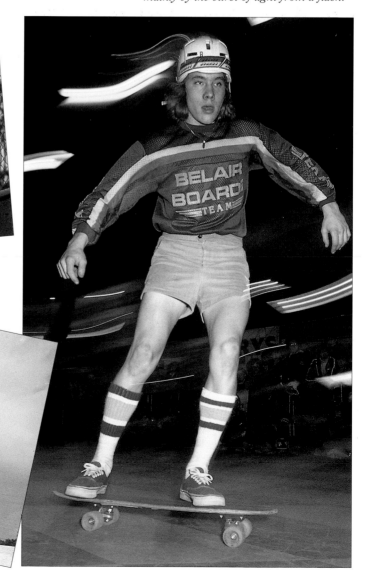

NATURE SAFARI

You don't have to be in the country to photograph nature. You can find many different types of wildlife in the most ordinary places. In fact, you can discover quite unexpected creatures, such as foxes, in towns and cities. In your garden, local park or on waste land, you will find a wide range of different plants and flowers. If there is water nearby, you may spot amphibians, such as frogs, toads and newts, as well as different species of birds and small animals. If you learn a little about their habits – such as where and when they like to feed – you will find it easier to capture some of these animal subjects on film. By setting up a feeding table in your garden, you will find that your subjects come to you.

You can use a compact camera with a zoom facility for many nature pictures, but to magnify subjects such as flowers or completely still animals, you will need to use an SLR or sophisticated compact that has a macro lens setting. A telephoto lens or zoom is also very useful because it means that you can stand well back from your subject so you don't frighten it, but you will still get a reasonably large image in your viewfinder.

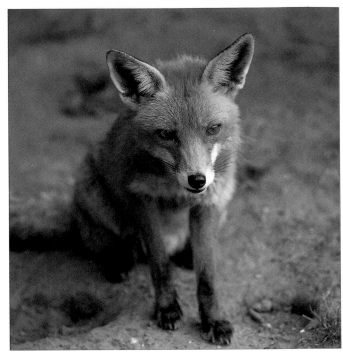

▲ Urban fox
To get a close-up effect with a compact camera, use a zoom if you have one, or get as close as you can then have part of the shot enlarged by the processor.

LOOK IT UP!
SLR lenses p 16, 90, 91
Animal portraits p 42 - 43
Macro lens p 90

▲ Run rabbit run
This photographer used a telephoto lens with a focal length of 200 mm to close in on a rabbit, which was hopping about on a piece of local waste land.

▲ Close-up colour
To focus on a subject less than 1 metre from the camera, such as this colourful butterfly, you will need to use an SLR or compact that has a macro setting.

▲ Froggy features
To get really good close-up nature shots, you will need to be very patient. Rest your camera against a support and be ready to shoot at just the right moment.

▼ Feeding time
If you hang a peanut feeder near to a window, you will be able to get close to your subjects without them seeing you.

If you want to encourage birds and small mammals into camera range, a good idea is to provide your potential subjects with a reliable source of food and water. Birds not only like bread, nuts and seeds, but many also enjoy scraps of meat and fat, especially in winter when it can be difficult to find food. Any mammals not in hibernation will also appreciate your gesture. When it is very cold, leave plenty of water out in shallow bowls, because most natural water supplies may be frozen over. If you set up a bird table, make sure it is in a place where you will have easy access with your camera, and plenty of natural cover to hide you from your subjects.

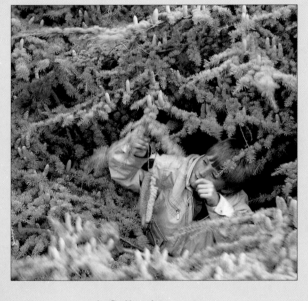

▲ Collecting cones
You can collect seeds, cones and berries to make your own bird feeders.

▶ Winter weather
If you put food out in snowy weather, you can guarantee that birds will stop for a welcome meal.

PHOTOGRAPHING BUILDINGS

As there are so many types and styles of building, from ancient cathedrals to giant skyscrapers, they offer endless opportunities for interesting photographs. You can take pictures of unusual details, such as doorways or windows, but if you want to photograph the whole structure it can be quite difficult to get far enough back. This is where a wide-angle lens is useful, as it allows you to photograph a larger area.

Even with a lens like this, you may have to point the camera up to avoid missing off the top of a building. Although this distorts the image, creating an effect known as 'converging verticals', this distortion can add impact to the photograph.

SLOPING VERTICALS

Taken from ground level with the camera pointed upwards, the sides of tall buildings seem to point inwards, or converge.

A solution is to move farther back, so that you don't have to angle the camera upwards, and use a telephoto lens for a larger image.

◄ Simple shrine
Although the building was not really attractive, this pretty shrine set into a wall made an effective detail shot.

► Doorway detail
Evening light, when the sun is low in the sky, was ideal to pick up the rich textures and colours of brick, wood, and stone in this medieval Italian street.

LOOK IT UP!

Cityscapes	p 62 - 63
Natural light	p 24 - 25
Wide-angle lens	p 16, 91
Composition	p 22 - 23

◄ Mirror image
This unusual composition captures the image of one building in the mirrored-glass wall of another. The reflection is made even more interesting because of the way the image of the building has been distorted. The photograph also contrasts two completely different architectural styles in one image.

▲ Dramatic angle
This stunning composition of an already dramatic building was taken in early evening. The warm tones of the light emphasize colour, and the unusual camera angle emphasizes height.

▲ Around the house
Don't forget that you can photograph your own home. If you compose the picture carefully and choose an interesting viewpoint, you can show something seen every day in a completely different way.

I Live Here

You can use your camera to record a personal view of your own home, told through the pictures you take of your favourite things, family and friends. Photograph your toys, books and pets, or just a corner of a room that tells a story. Include pictures of people in your collection, maybe in situations that you see regularly.

We often take for granted the things we see every day, so look very carefully at familiar surroundings. Take some close-up pictures. You will find that they often bring to light small features that you wouldn't normally notice. Make use of any interesting lighting, such as sunlight coming through a window.

LOOK IT UP!
Natural light p 24–25
Still life p 70–73
People portraits p 38–41

► **Candid camera**
This is the photographer's sister sitting at her desk as she does every day.

▲ **Bedroom clutter**
Don't tidy up your room for this project. It is supposed to show things as they really are – mess and all.

▲ **Hide-and-seek**
A telephoto lens captured a friend in the garden in the middle of a game of hide-and-seek.

◀ Posing people
You can take 'posed' pictures, like this one of two young friends, as well as more natural shots.

▲ Green fingers
The photographer grew all the plants and seedlings shown here.

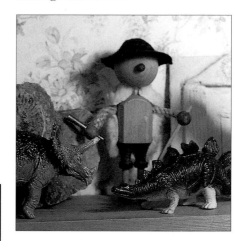

▲ Toy friends
The photographer's collection of toys, arranged on a bedroom shelf, is a perfect subject for this project.

◀ Glowing globe
This globe is one of the photographer's favourite possessions. When illuminated, it creates an interesting lighting effect.

PHOTO STORY

A PHOTO story is a detailed, informative series of pictures. They are usually created by photo-journalists, who record events purely through photographs. The pictures may show an occasion or activity, or record the daily routine of someone who has an interesting occupation.

For this project you will become a photo-journalist. Choose a subject you are interested in or record a day in the life of someone you know. This photographer followed a fly fisherman for a day and, like a photojournalist, experimented with different camera angles and positions to create a varied collection of different shots.

Your final pictures should tell the viewer all about the events that you have photographed, without needing any words at all.

▼ Setting the scene
This attractive landscape establishes the scene for the whole activity by giving it a background setting. It gives further information by showing the special waterproof clothing the fisherman wears to wade into the river.

▲ Fishing tackle
Most experienced fly fishermen make their own 'flies'. These are insect-shaped lures that attract the fish to the hook. This opening shot is full of interesting detail, which captures the viewer's attention. It immediately outlines the difference between this and other types of fishing, and invites the viewer to find out more.

▲ Detailed activity
This shot focuses in on the fisherman's hands as he attaches the flies to his line. Although you cannot see his face, you get a sense of the concentration involved.

▲ Camera close-up
To get just the right image, you will have to experiment with camera angles and positions. This close-up shows in detail the flies the fisherman has created.

► The punchline
Every good story – in words or pictures – needs to have a punchy ending. The obvious way to conclude a coverage of a day's fishing expedition is with a picture of a fish in the fisherman's net. The photographer took the picture from directly overhead, giving the impression of looking straight into the net.

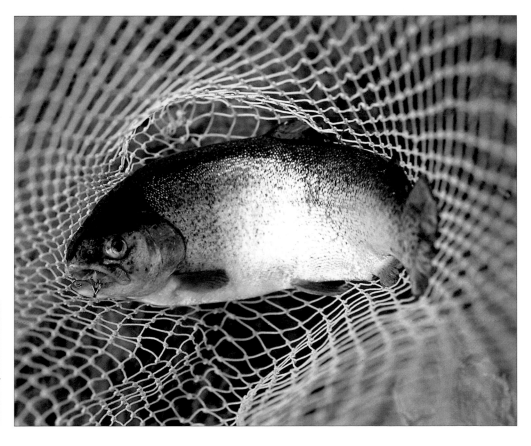

LOOK IT UP!

People portraits p 38–41

Close-ups p 60–63

SLR equipment p 16

Still life p 70–73

HOLIDAY PHOTOGRAPHS

HOLIDAYS are a perfect time to practise your photography. You can discover many colourful and exciting subjects when you visit a new place. Use your camera to record images of different lifestyles, interesting architecture and unusual shops and markets. A panorama could be used to record a particularly stunning view and you should find opportunities for some candid shots.

Don't load yourself down with too much equipment. A camera with a zoom lens is ideal because it can take wide views as well as detailed close-ups. If you are going somewhere sunny and hot, you can take a slower ISO 100 film.

HOLIDAY PHOTOGRAPHY CHECKLIST

● Keep equipment to a minimum.
● Don't leave your camera in hot sunshine for long periods, or the film may spoil.
● When you are on the beach, make sure that sand doesn't get into the camera – it may jam the inner workings or scratch the lens.
● Look for details of buildings such as windows and doors to give variety to your photographs.
● Take candid shots in markets, or action shots if you visit a beach or water park.
● Get up early to capture local atmosphere and colour when shops and markets prepare for the day.

◀ ◀ ▲ People watching
You should find lots of opportunities for candid shots like this (left). But if you have time, and your subjects don't object, try taking a more considered, informal portrait (above and far left).

LOOK IT UP!

SLR equipment p 16, 90

Panorama p 64–65

People portraits p 38–41

Landscapes and cityscapes p 60–63

Film speed p 18,19

Photographing buildings p 50–51

◀ ▲ Display details
When you visit another country, look out for displays of unusual subjects. Move in close to take the picture and crop out all the surrounding detail to add impact to the composition.

▲ ▶ Getting in close
Close-up shots such as these emphasize colour and shape. Street markets are an excellent source of close-up and still life subjects (right). In the countryside, look out for colourful scenes like this field of giant sunflowers (above).

▲ Earth bound
Look downwards – crazy paving or sun-baked earth like this is a perfect subject for an abstract image. It will provide an unusual textural reminder of your holiday.

▲ Instant sunshine
Look for interesting detail on houses and other buildings. This scene of flowering pot plants against a rough, sun-baked wall and tiled roof is full of Mediterranean sunshine.

▶ Off the wall
If you see a group of likely subjects, such as these men sitting on a wall, don't hesitate to take a quick candid shot.

▼ Furry friends
Animals can also provide reminders of your holiday. This black-and-white study is of the hotel owner's cat.

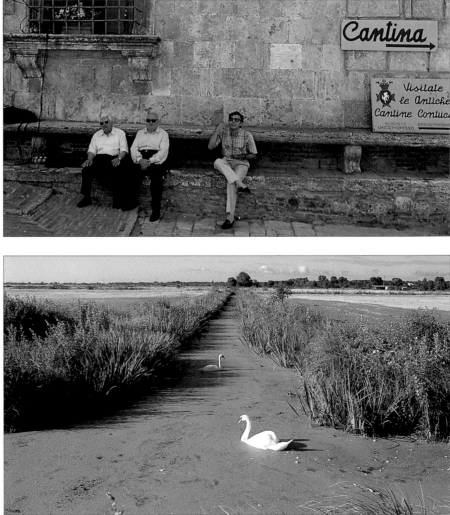

▶ In the country
Pictures of the surrounding countryside can show another aspect of the place you have visited. This well-balanced composition is bursting with strong, natural colours, and the swans provide a perfect point of focus.

▼ ▶ Dramatic duo
In both shots, picture shape complements the subject. Below, the emphasis is on the converging verticals of the building. The waterfall (right) is framed by trees.

▼ Seaside studies
These simple studies give a real feeling of the seaside. This seagull (below left) was snapped with a telephoto lens. The boy (below) was perfect for a candid shot.

LANDSCAPES AND CITYSCAPES

APART from photographs of family and friends, landscapes are one of the most popular subjects for the camera. A stunning landscape can make a great picture, and there are plenty of different locations to choose from. Country landscape scenes can range from a patchwork of fields to snowy mountain peaks. Parks and nature reserves offer plenty of opportunities, too. But landscapes also include city views – often called cityscapes – and these can be just as dramatic.

Natural light plays an important part in landscape photography. The sun moves through the sky during the day and this creates a variety of different lighting effects. A good time for landscape photographs is often in the early morning or the late afternoon. At these times of day the sun is low in the sky and the angle of its light tends to make colours look darker and richer. The landscape seems to be full of interesting shadows and textures. Light also alters with the seasons and with the weather, so these will change the appearance of the landscape too. One of the secrets of successful landscape photography is always to keep one eye on the weather and the other on the clock. Be ready to set off to photograph a favourite scene when you think the conditions are right. Bad weather doesn't necessarily mean bad photographs; some of the very best landscape pictures have been taken in stormy weather – but not usually when it's actually raining.

POSITIONING THE HORIZON

The horizon line is where the sky meets the land. In most landscape photographs you can see the horizon, and part of creating a good composition is deciding where it should be in your picture. If you point the camera down, the horizon appears near the top of the frame (1). This makes the picture look closed in, and also gives you a lot of foreground. If you point the camera up, the horizon is towards the bottom of the frame (2). This shows a lot more sky and gives a feeling of space in the photograph. Both of these are more dramatic images than the final picture (3), where the horizon is in the middle of the frame.

1. High horizon line

2. Low horizon line

3. Mid horizon line

▲ Stormy light
In this picture the lines of hills either side of the trees guide the eye towards them. Their strong, bleak shapes are an important part of the composition. The photographer waited for the sun to shine through the storm clouds before he took the picture.

◀ ▲ Moving water
Moving water, such as fountains or waterfalls, can either be recorded with a fast shutter speed, so that its motion is 'frozen', or a slow speed, so that the water blurs while the picture is being taken. In the first picture (left) a shutter speed of 1/500 second was used, and in the other (above) a shutter speed of 1/15 second was used, with the camera held on a tripod to keep it steady.

Knowing what will be the best lighting for your chosen scene is just as important for town and city photographs as for country landscapes. These 'cityscape' pictures are just as rich in interest, colour, tone, texture, and pattern as their country counterparts, and it is the quality and direction of light that emphasizes or tones down all of these aspects. The sky is one of the most important elements in a landscape or cityscape shot. Early in the morning, or towards dusk, when the sun is not far above the horizon, the sky can be full of fabulous fiery colours, and clouds can look extremely dramatic. A sky like this, seen above the silhouetted shapes of tall city buildings, perhaps with low sunlight glinting off a few high windows, could be a winning photograph.

Early evening or night photography is also interesting to explore. Once shop windows, car headlights, and streetlighting are lit up, an ordinary scene can be transformed into a fairy-tale image. You can make these light sources produce strange colours and distortions using normal daylight-balanced film, or you can pan the camera to achieve a sense of movement and action. As the night sky becomes darker, you will almost certainly need a tripod or some flat surface to steady the camera during exposure times that could last for many seconds.

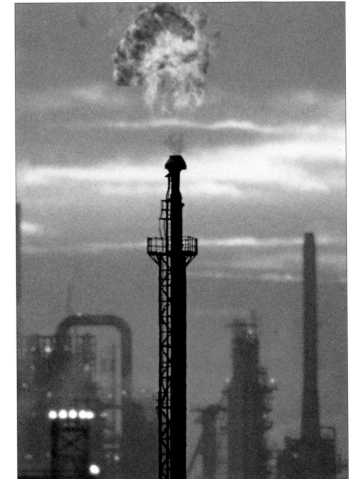

▲ **Hot and cold**
The muted greys of this industrial scene contrast with the fiery hues of the gas flare and the sky.

LOOK IT UP!

Panorama p 64–65

Montage p 66–69

Natural light p 24–25

▲ **Perfect harmony**
The striking colours of the truck and the bridge, the sky and the river, all harmonize together.

55 mm focal length

▶ **Same position, different views**
The advantage of having an SLR camera, or a compact with a good zoom lens, is that you have a range of lens focal lengths to choose from so you can achieve a variety of viewpoints. The series of pictures on the right were taken with a zoom lens set at different focal lengths. The photographer pivoted the camera around from the same position to record a visit to the local park.

▲ ▲ ► Changing light

The direction and quality of the light striking your subject can completely change its appearance. Here is the same mountain shot at different times of the day. The first picture was taken early in the morning and shows the sun illuminating every detail of the mountain's craggy surface. The next shot was taken in late afternoon, with mist diffusing the sunlight and creating a more moody picture. In the final picture, taken at dusk, the mountain is backlit and appears as a silhouette against a dramatic, late evening sky.

70 mm focal length

90 mm focal length

210 mm focal length

PANORAMAS

Sᴏᴍᴇᴛɪᴍᴇꜱ a scene can be so wide that you have to turn your whole body to take it all in. It can be quite a problem to capture a view like this on film. If your camera has a wide-angle lens or zoom setting, and you stand far enough back, you might just about fit the whole scene in. But on the print, the details will be so small that the picture will lose its impact.

A professional photographer might have a special panoramic camera for situations like this. The lens on this camera swivels as it takes the picture and produces a very long negative. But you can get the same effect by taking a series of pictures from the same spot and sticking them together afterwards. This is called a panorama. You will need to support your camera, or use a tripod, to keep the camera steady. You can even make a picture that covers 360° – a complete circle.

▲ ▶ **Wide-angle comparison**
This single picture (above) was taken with a wide-angle 28 mm lens. Although it takes in a lot of the scene, it doesn't capture the whole sweep of land as in the panoramic version (top right).
The wide-angle lens also makes the subject details look small and unimpressive.

Image 1

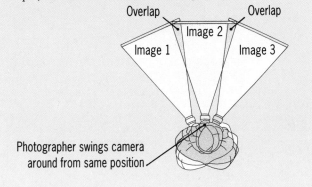

SHOOTING A PANORAMA

Choose a panoramic scene to photograph, then find a level surface, such as a wall or post, which you can use to steady the camera.

1 *Position the camera for your picture. Take the first shot, then swivel the camera round to the next part of the scene. Include a slight overlap, as this will act as a guide when you put the prints together. Repeat to cover the complete scene.*

2 *When your prints are returned, match up the overlaps to recreate the view. Carefully stick the prints together. You can either trim the tops and bottoms or leave them in 'steps', like the ones shown on these pages.*

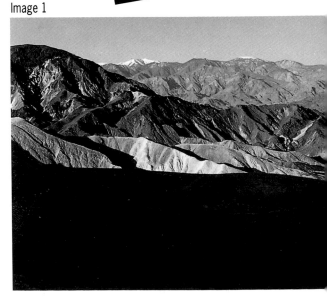

Overlap　　　　　Overlap
Image 2
Image 1　　　　　Image 3

Photographer swings camera
around from same position

▼ Urban view
This canal scene is framed by trees and bushes, which give scale and depth to the picture.

▼ Grand scene
A panorama captures the whole of this stunning view of the Grand Canyon.

Overlap   Image 2   Overlap

Image 3

MONTAGE

A SIMILAR technique to panorama is montage. This sort of photographic compilation is a bit like a jigsaw. Instead of just joining photographs together in a long strip, you make a patchwork of pictures. These will cover both the length and depth of the scene. The advantage of this technique is that it shows a much wider area of picture than a panorama.

There are no rules with montage. You can simply mount the finished prints on a piece of stiff cardboard for display, trimming the edges to fit a frame or leaving them to make an interesting irregular shape. You don't need to decide until you have assembled your prints, then you will see which suits the subject best.

HOW TO SHOOT A MONTAGE

1 Stand in one spot and take your photographs in a systematic way to ensure you cover the whole scene.

2 To avoid gaps in the finished montage, overlap adjoining areas that contain important details.

3 Miss out areas, such as broad expanses of cloudless sky, but keep the horizon as it gives continuity.

4 Assemble your finished prints. Overlap the pictures to cover the length and depth of the scene.

LOOK IT UP!

Photographing
buildings p 50-51

People portraits p 38–41

Panoramas p 64–65

▲ **Distorted view**
In this montage, featuring details of a fishing boat, the photographer was not trying to create a recognizable, real-life subject. Parts of the scene, like the mast and crow's nest, were repeated many times, but each was shot from a slightly different angle.

▲ **Split image**
This unusual montage was made from a single photograph of a Chinese pagoda. This was then cut into pieces and these were rearranged to create an interesting abstract image.

◀ **Modern architecture**
For this montage of office buildings, the photographer shot from close-up, far away, and from different angles. Modern architecture offers many opportunities for dramatic montage pictures, as the repeated shapes can be easily distorted by moving the prints slightly out of line.

▲ Group montage

A professional photographer might have a special camera with a lens that rotates as it takes the picture to include a long row of people in the same shot. You can get a similar effect and add depth to your scene by carefully taking a series of photographs and joining them together as a patchwork. If you look carefully at the picture above, you can see that the same person has been included at both the beginning and the end of the group. This adds an extra touch of humour to this already interesting montage.

If you mount your prints in an album, without flipping the pages over you can only see a few pictures at a time. If you have a collection of prints, perhaps of a special occasion or group, you can create a montage that can be framed to hang on a wall. This type of montage is made up of many separate prints, each with its own complete image. Photographs taken on holiday, at home, and at Christmas time and other occasions all go to make an interesting and a varied montage.

MAKE A FRAMED MONTAGE

1 *Collect pictures with different backgrounds, colours and views to give variety. Position your first picture roughly in the middle of the space.*

2 *Arrange the other images around your first one. As you can see here, these pictures will start to define the overall shape of the montage.*

Subjects positioned in a circle

Direction of camera swing

Arrange your subjects in a circle around you, as shown here. Stand in exactly the same spot, but swivel to take each picture. In this way your subjects will always be the same distance from the camera. When the shots are joined together, the group will look like they were standing in a row.

▶ **Facial montage**
An unusual idea for a montage is to take pictures of the faces of each member of your family. Join details from each person together to make a single picture or family portrait.

3 *Now you can start filling in the gaps. It doesn't matter if pictures overlap, as long as you are careful not to cover up any important details.*

4 *When the montage is assembled and you are happy with all the pictures, lift each one carefully, apply adhesive, and stick it into position. The finished montage in this example has been framed, but you could pin the pictures on to a pinboard.*

STILL LIFE

STILL life photographs are of objects, not people or places. There are no rules about which objects to use, but those that have something in common – such as colour, texture, or shape – often work well together. You will find that even the most ordinary things make good subjects.

Rearrange the objects you choose until you are happy with the way they look. You will have to experiment with different lighting and camera angles to get the best results. The background to your subject is also very important. Choose a setting carefully so that it complements the subject but doesn't distract the eye.

Indoor set-up

Most still life photography is done like this (right), on a convenient surface such as a tabletop. The objects to be photographed are placed on a piece of coloured or white background paper, which is bent upwards, behind the subject to create a single, continuous surface. The main light source is natural daylight coming in through a nearby window. A reflector has been used on the far side of the objects to reflect some of the window light back into the shadows and so lighten them a little. The camera is mounted on a tripod. This leaves the photographer free to arrange the objects and check the composition through the viewfinder.

Window light

Background paper

Reflector

'G'-clamp

Reflective surface

Stand

▲ Good enough to eat
These pieces of fruit make effective still life subjects. Natural daylight was used to light the image, and the colour and surface detail of the old, wooden tabletop enhance the picture without distracting the eye from the subjects.

▲ Making a reflector
This simple reflector made from white card can be used to reflect light and direct it into areas that are in shadow.

▲ Flower power

For a dramatic image, show your subject large in the frame. In the picture above, tight framing emphasizes the vibrant colours of the flowers, which were lit by natural light from a window.

◄ ▼ ▼ Tabletop tips

These three pictures were all taken using the simple tabletop set-up shown on the opposite page. All of the arrangements fill the frame without looking cluttered. For the colourful close-up (below left), a macro lens setting was also used.

LOOK IT UP!
Reflector p 90
Macro lens p 90
Depth of field p 21, 43, 88

Discovering a still life

You can find interesting arrangements of objects almost anywhere – around your home, out in the garden, or in the street. These make perfect ready-made set-ups for still life shots. Look out for interesting patterns, contrasting or harmonizing colours, or a collection of complementary shapes. In some cases, you might want to make minor alterations to the arrangement, but you will find many subjects that don't need any rearrangement at all.

▲ Fallen apples
You can crop an image to suit the subject. Here the picture shape echoes the line of the garden tools, leading your eye down to the apples at the bottom of the picture.

LOOK IT UP!

Composition p 22–23

Close-ups p 76–77

Natural light p 24–25

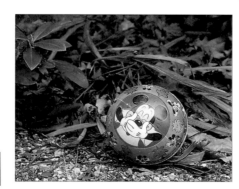

▲ Colour contrasts
The bright primary colours of this ball contrast with the dull greens and browns of the background setting.

▲ Autumn leaves
The two photographs above reflect the feel of autumn. The rusty metal in the top picture blends with the muted autumn shades. The mass of colour in the picture below provides a perfect background for fallen leaves.

Out and about

Look out for potentially interesting still life subjects. Shop windows are always a rich source, as shopkeepers arrange their goods to appeal to the passer-by. Display stands are often full of repeated shapes and bright colours. Even bicycles, propped up and awaiting their owners' return, can make an unusual composition.

SPECIAL EFFECTS

WHEN you take pictures, you usually want your finished prints to look as much like the original subject as possible. But you can use special effects to enhance an image, or make it look visually interesting rather than immediately recognizable. Many effects can be achieved simply and without any extra cost. For others, such as colour changes, you may need to buy special attachments for your camera.

◄ Mirror magic
This clever special effect was achieved by photographing a reflection, rather than the neon sign itself, in the mirrored glass wall of a building.

▼ Using patterned glass
The photographer took this intriguing picture through the type of heavily patterned glass you often find in a front door. The subject, although very distorted, is a pathway and gate.

Effects with filters

Soft focus

You can buy special soft-focus filters that have a grid of very fine lines engraved on their surface. However, you can achieve a similar effect simply by stretching a piece of stocking material over the lens itself or over an ordinary UV filter.

UV filter ___

Mesh ___

Rubber band ___

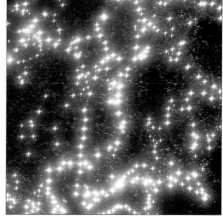

▲ Christmas lights – without filter
Before the filter is added, the lights, although distinct, have little impact.

▲ Christmas lights – with filter
Stocking material stretched over a UV filter creates a soft, blurred effect.

Smeared image effect

For an image that is very obviously distorted, smear petroleum jelly over plain glass or a UV filter. The more jelly, the more distorted the result. Never put petroleum jelly on the glass of the lens itself.

Cotton bud

Petroleum jelly

UV filter

▲ Flowers – without filter
Without the filter, this is a very attractive still life of sunflowers.

▲ Flowers – with filter
This jelly-smeared UV filter makes the flower look as if it were rotating.

Special effect filters

Gelatine special effect filters are cheap to buy. A wide range of effects are available, including many different colours, some with a clear centre spot and others that graduate from dark to light. You need a filter holder to attach one to your camera lens and these are available for SLRs and compacts.

Filter holder

Filter glass

Tobacco graduated filter

CLOSE-UPS

THE great thing about close-up photography is that you can reveal a subject, or part of a subject, in a way that may never have been seen before. One of the best places to practise this technique is at home. The most ordinary of subjects can look mysterious or intriguing when viewed really close up.

You cannot focus most compact cameras on a subject that is closer than a metre from the camera. To take very close shots, you will need to use an SLR or compact camera that has a macro lens setting to magnify your subject. The objects used for the close-up pictures on these pages are everyday kitchen utensils, and are shown in the photograph below.

▲ Odd ones out
Can you spot the objects in this picture shown in close-up on these pages?

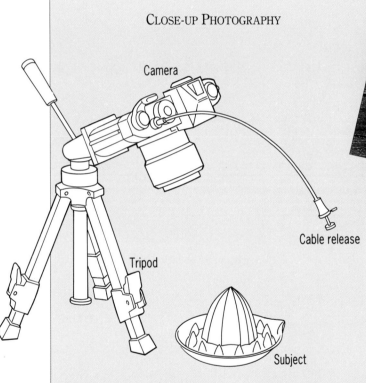

CLOSE-UP PHOTOGRAPHY

Camera

Cable release

Tripod

Subject

Many modern lenses have a 'macro' setting. This allows the lens to focus closer to the subject than usual. Depth of field is always extremely shallow when taking close-ups, so you will need to select your smallest aperture to increase the zone of sharp focus. Using small apertures usually means selecting a slow shutter speed to compensate (unless the subject is very bright and you are using a fast film), so a tripod is essential to prevent camera shake. Firing the shutter with a cable release is also essential so that you don't jar the camera as you release the shutter.

◀ ▼ ▼ ▲ Strangely familiar
As you can see from these photographs, by concentrating on a particular part of an object in close-up, you can draw attention to texture, shape and colour. Unusual camera angles and lighting effects will add impact to your pictures.

LOOK IT UP!

Cable release p 16
Macro lens p 90
Tripod p 91
Abstract designs p 78–79

ABSTRACT DESIGNS

ABSTRACT photography is all about looking at objects in a totally different way. Rather than photographing the whole object, an abstract view usually highlights or emphasizes one aspect, such as colour, texture or pattern, by concentrating on a detail. You will find subjects in the most unusual places, but you will have to look very carefully. Industrial areas in particular are full of great photo opportunities.

PHOTOGRAMS

A photogram is a print made directly from the subject itself, and is produced by placing objects on top of a piece of printing paper and exposing them to light. You will get a more even image if you use an enlarger, but you can use natural light, although the finished photogram will not be quite as sharp.

Step 1
If you are working in a darkroom, place a piece of printing paper on the enlarger baseboard, emulsion-side up, and arrange your objects on its surface. If you are using natural light, place your objects on the paper in complete darkness.

Step 2
Set the enlarger lens to about f8 and give an exposure of 15 seconds, or expose the printing paper to natural light. Where the objects block the light, the paper stays white; where the light reaches the paper, it will turn grey or black.

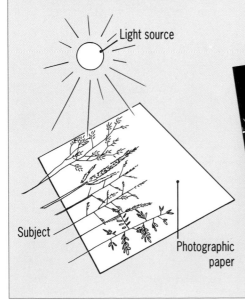

Light source

Subject

Photographic paper

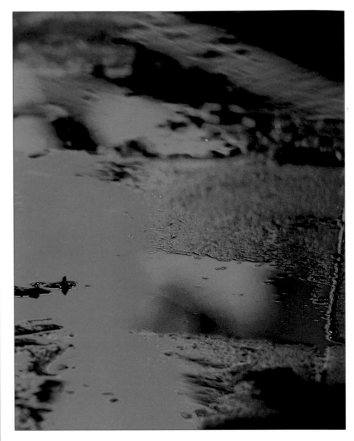

▲ Road reflections
Tight framing has turned this night-time reflection of neon lights in the wet surface of a road into a luminous dazzle of abstract colour.

▲ Rough rope
You can almost feel the rough texture of this rope, which is highlighted by the sun.

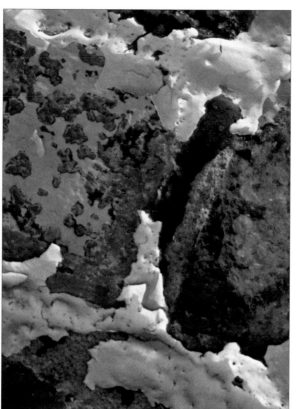

◄ Crumbling paint
Moving in close has isolated this small section of crumbling paint and the underlying brick. Setting the camera at an angle has helped to emphasize the picture's abstract qualities.

LOOK IT UP!
Making a print p 30-31, 88
Photographic paper p G
Close-ups p 76–77
Special effects p 74–75
SLR equipment p 16

▼ Splash of colour
A detail of a metal door splashed with paint provides an interesting contrast of colours and textures.

SELF-PORTRAITS

TAKING self-portraits can be a lot of fun. There are several techniques you can use, but for most you will need to put the camera on a firm surface, or use a tripod. You can use a self-timer if you have this facility on your camera. The ten-second delay after you press the shutter-release button gives you time to position yourself. Alternatively, use a cable release, which is an extension cable that triggers the shutter when you press a plunger. This will also enable you to stand away from the camera, and still take a picture. Other techniques are using a mirror and holding the camera at arm's length.

▲ Clowning around
A self-portrait doesn't have to show you as you appear every day. By dressing up you can change your image completely.

▲ Cyclist friends
You don't have to leave yourself out of group shots. The photographer joined the cyclist group in this picture by using the camera's self-timer.

▲ Feet first
A self-portrait doesn't have to include your face. The subject of this picture is the photographer's own feet, as seen from a sitting position.

SELF-PORTRAIT SKILLS

● Position the camera on a convenient, flat surface, and look through the viewfinder. Make sure you are happy with the surroundings you will appear in.
● Autofocus cameras are easy to use for self-portraits. But you must make sure that you stand in the target area (this is usually in the middle of the viewfinder).
● With a manual camera, prefocus on an object that is the same distance from the camera as you will be when the picture is taken.

◄ **Dramatic lighting**
This picture was taken using a cable release (seen in the photographer's hand). A sunbeam acts as a spotlight, leaving much of the picture in shadow.

LOOK IT UP!
Natural light p 24–25
People portraits p 38–41
Cable release p 16
Self-timer p 90
Parallax error p 20

▼ **Using a prop**
Although this is a self-portrait, by holding a second camera as a prop, the photographer has made the picture appear as if it were taken by somebody else.

◄ **Mirror image**
If you are using a mirror to take a self-portrait, the camera must be mounted on a tripod, or supported, because you will need to use a slow shutter speed to compensate for the lack of light. If you don't want the camera to appear in the picture, put it at an angle to one side of the mirror, out of shot.

DISPLAYING YOUR PICTURES

You have taken lots of photographs. You may even have developed and printed some of them yourself. But unless you display your pictures, no one else will be able to enjoy them. There are lots of ways you can present your pictures. The simplest way is to put them into albums. This will also protect your pictures and keep them clean. Keep a different album for each subject. If you frame your prints, either in shop-bought or home-made frames, you can hang them on a wall. But remember that you don't need to frame the whole of the picture; you can crop it to give the image more impact. This section of the book shows you how to use 'L-shapes' to choose a suitable section of the print. Finally, you will find information on how to take your interest further – through courses, exhibitions, books and magazines – plus some useful addresses for further information on different aspects of photography.

PICTURE PRESENTATION

Y OU will soon build up a collection of photographs that you are proud of. There are lots of ways you can display them. This makes them easier to view and allows other people to enjoy them, too. Photo albums are useful for storing lots of pictures and for carrying them around. Your favourite prints can even be enlarged and framed, or you could turn them into greetings cards for family or friends.

Enlarged print album

Flip album

Self-adhesive, spiral-bound album

Types of photo album

Photo albums come in all shapes and sizes, from small pocket types to large, book-sized albums that can hold up to a hundred prints. Some albums require corner mounts, others are self-adhesive with a protective plastic top sheet that holds the prints securely in place. Enlarged prints have more impact, and special albums are made for prints of up to about 20 x 25 cm (far left). The range of albums for the various sizes of print include this handy 80-picture flip-up design (top left) as well as large-format albums with rigid pages (below left).

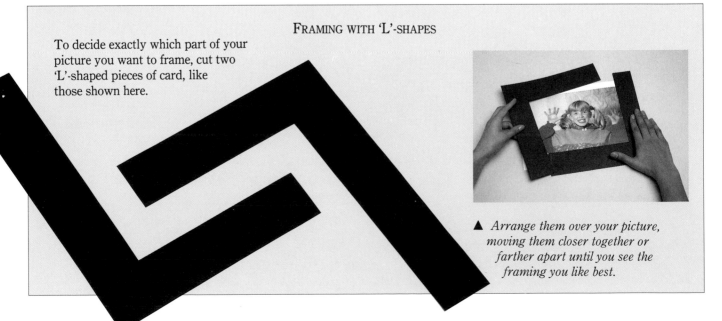

FRAMING WITH 'L'-SHAPES

To decide exactly which part of your picture you want to frame, cut two 'L'-shaped pieces of card, like those shown here.

▲ *Arrange them over your picture, moving them closer together or farther apart until you see the framing you like best.*

Making a photocard

1 *Gather together all the materials and equipment you need to make and decorate your photocard, together with the print you intend to use.*

2 *Fold a piece of card in half. Mark the position of the print on the front and cut out the centre of the card to make a frame.*

3 *Attach the print to the inside of the card frame with sticky tape or glue. Now your card is ready to decorate.*

4 *Decorate your card frame with anything you wish. Use a colour or a decorative theme that complements the picture, or suits the occasion.*

◀ **Photocard ideas**
Photocards are a fun way to use your pictures. You can use them for any occasion – birthdays, weddings or Christmas. Decorate your cards with anything you like to give an interesting design. Wallpaper and wrapping paper are useful. You can even add glitter and stars.

Mounting and framing

You will find a huge variety of ready-made frames in the shops. They range in price and quality, as well as size. You can also discover very attractive antique frames if you visit second-hand shops. But whichever frame you choose, careful and accurate mounting will make your picture look even better.

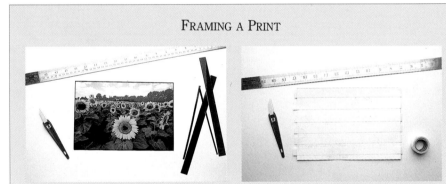

◀ ▲ Frame styles

These are a few examples of the many different frames that you can buy. They range from those with fancy cast metal borders, to simple perspex clip frames.

FRAMING A PRINT

1 *Using a sharp craft knife and a metal ruler, trim your print neatly. Make sure that the final border is straight and even all the way around.*

2 *Turn the print face down and place strips of double-sided tape at regular intervals across the back of the print. Trim off any excess tape.*

3 *Cut a piece of mounting board to the size of the frame you are using. Peel the backing paper off the tape and carefully place the print in position.*

4 *Smooth the print down so that it is perfectly flat. Place the mounted print on the backing board, and position the glass on top. Clip them all together.*

FINDING OUT MORE

Many schools run photography clubs that you can join after school. This will give you access to school photographic facilities and a darkroom, as well as giving you an opportunity to further your learning with other people who share your interest. If there isn't an established club, why not form your own? Contact your form teacher and you may find that a member of staff is interested and willing to help. Local authorities often run evening classes, although these may have age restrictions.

When you leave school at 16 or 18 you can go on to college or university to study photography at a higher level. This is generally the way to start if you want to become a professional photographer.

Photographic exhibitions

Many large cities and towns will have photographic exhibitions at regular intervals during the year. Some galleries specialize in photography and have exhibitions of different photographers' work running all the time. Keep an eye on the 'events' column of your local newspaper or, failing that, the magazine *British Journal of Photography* lists major photographic exhibitions throughout the country. You could also try at your local library for a book entitled *Directory of Exhibition Spaces*, which lists permanent gallery and exhibition venues in England, Scotland, Wales and Northern Ireland.

Books and magazines

There are many well-written and beautifully illustrated books on photography. Some concentrate on the technical side of the subject, others on aesthetics. Try your local library, which will have a section on photography. You could save up for any books that are particularly useful or perhaps ask your parents for them as birthday presents.

Magazines are another excellent source of information on photography.They are usually published weekly or monthly, and nearly all review the latest in photographic equipment. Many hold photographic competitions with different categories of entry to suit different age groups. If you feel confident about some of your photographs, you should try your luck and enter. Most will return your prints to you if you include a stamped, self-addressed envelope.

Useful addresses

You may find the following addresses useful for general information, bookshop facilities, exhibitions, or photographic workshops.

The Royal Photographic Society
The Octagon
Milsom Street
Bath BA1 1DN
0225 462841

Photofusion
17A Electric Lane
Brixton
London SW19 8LA
071 738 5774

Ffotoworks and Ffotogallery
31 Charles Street
Cardiff CF1 4EB
0222 387560

F stop gallery and Darkroom
Green Park Station
Bath BA1 1JB
0225 316922

National Museum of Photography,
Film and Television
Pictureville
Bradford BD5 0TR
0274 727488

The Photographer's Gallery
5&8 Great Newport Street
London WC2H 7HY
071 240 1969

GLOSSARY

A

Abstract image
An image that is non-realistic, usually concentrating on an aspect of a subject, rather than the subject as a whole. This is often achieved by photographing just a small part.

Angle of view
The amount of a scene that can be taken in by a lens. A wide-angle lens has a wider angle of view than a telephoto lens.

Aperture
The opening behind the lens, usually within the lens barrel, that allows light into the camera to expose the film. The size of the opening can be made smaller to allow less light in when light levels are high, or larger to allow more light in when light levels are low.

Autoexposure
An automatic system found on most modern cameras. It adjusts the aperture size and the shutter speed, to ensure correct exposure.

Autofocus
An automatic system found on many compact and SLR cameras. It adjusts the focus setting of the lens to produce a sharp image.

B

Backlight compensation button
A control found on some cameras that opens the lens aperture up to allow extra light into the camera when the subject is lit from behind. This compensates for the fact that the side of the subject facing the lens will be in shadow.

Backlighting
A type of lighting effect that occurs when the subject is positioned between the sun and the camera.

C

Camera obscura
An early drawing aid. Originally a darkened room with a tiny hole in one outside wall. Light entering the room through the hole would project an upside-down image of the scene outside onto the opposite wall. This image could then be traced onto paper or canvas.

Colour cast
An unnatural, overall colour on a print or slide. This can happen if you bounce light from a flash gun off a coloured wall, or use daylight-balanced film in electric light.

Compact camera
A small, highly automatic camera with a lens that cannot be removed and changed for another. The viewfinder is separate to the lens.

Contrast
The difference between the brightest and darkest parts of a picture.

Converging verticals
A trick of perspective that makes vertical parallel lines seem to converge as they get farther away from the camera.

Cropping
Changing the camera position or the focal length of the lens to select certain parts of a scene. You can also crop in on a negative when making a print, or crop a print by cutting or mounting it.

D

Darkroom
A light-tight room where film is processed and prints are made.

Daylight-balanced film
Colour film that is designed to give accurate subject colours when exposed by daylight or by flash.

Depth of field
The zone of sharp focus in a picture. Depth of field varies depending on the lens aperture, the lens focal length, and where the lens is focused. Small apertures have a greater depth of field than large ones; wide-angle lenses have a greater depth of field than telephoto lenses; and depth of field becomes greater the farther away the lens is focused.

Developer
A processing chemical used with film and printing paper that converts the invisible image, present in the photographic emulsion, into an image that can be seen.

Diffused light
Light that has passed through some type of semi-opaque material, such as tissue paper or gauze, and so has been scattered.

E

Emulsion
The light-sensitive coating on film or paper that records the image of the subject. The emulsion consists of crystals of silver halides mixed with gelatine.

Enlarger
The piece of equipment used in a darkroom to make enlarged prints from film. It has its own light source and lens, and projects an image of the film down onto a baseboard where the printing paper is positioned.

'En' print
The standard, album-sized enlargement that is produced by most automatic processing and printing machines.

Exposure
The amount of light received by a piece of film or printing paper. In a camera, exposure is controlled by a combination of the aperture size and the length of time the shutter remains open (the shutter speed).

Exposure meter
A light-sensitive device in a camera, linked to both the lens aperture and the shutter, that controls the film exposure. In non-automatic SLR cameras, the exposure meter displays aperture size and shutter speed recommendations for the photographer to set manually.

F

Fast film
Film that is very sensitive to light and is used when lighting conditions are dim. Fast films have large ISO numbers, such as ISO 1600 or 3200.

Film clip
Weighted clips that are attached to the top and bottom of a roll of processed and washed film so that it can be hung up to dry. The weight prevents the film from curling as it dries.

Film pressure plate
A sprung metal or plastic plate on the inside surface of a camera's back. When closed, this presses the film perfectly flat before exposure.

Filter
A glass disc, or a piece of plastic or gelatine, that fits over the front of a camera lens and is designed to alter the colour or appearance of the image.

Fixer
A processing chemical that makes the remaining unexposed silver halides on film or paper soluble. This means that they can then be washed away, leaving the film insensitive to light.

Flash
A portable form of artificial light used mainly indoors, at night, or when there is not enough light during the day for a successful exposure. Many compact cameras have a built-in flash, but SLR cameras usually need a flash gun to be attached.

Floppy disk
A magnetic disk that stores information. In a still video camera, the disk records the different intensities and other characteristics of the light rays entering the lens. When the camera is linked to a television set, the disk displays full-colour pictures.

Focal length
A lens measurement describing the distance between the back of the lens and the film. A lens that has a long focal length, such as a telephoto lens, increases the size of the image in the frame. A lens with a short focal length, such as a wide-angle lens, decreases the size of the image in the frame. Focal length is usually measured in millimetres.

Focusing
Moving the lens either closer to, or farther away from the film in order to produce a sharp image.

F stop or f number
A series of numbers engraved on the control ring of a lens. They indicate the size of the lens aperture. Moving to the next largest f number (f8 to f11, for example) makes the aperture smaller. Moving to the next smallest (f5.6 to f4, for example) makes the aperture larger.

I

Image
A photographic representation of a real scene or object.

ISO
An abbreviation for International Standards Organization. An international system for rating the speed of film.

L

Large-format camera
A type of camera used mainly by professional photographers. They produce pictures on large, individual, sheets of film, which are loaded into the camera one at a time.

Large-format film
The individual sheets of film used in a large-format camera.

Lens
A single piece of specially-shaped glass, or a series of pieces of glass, that focus the light rays entering the camera onto the film.

Lens hood
A cup-shaped attachment, made from rubber or metal, that fits around the front of a lens. Used mainly on SLR cameras, this prevents bright light, usually the sun, from shining directly into the lens and causing flare.

Light rays
In photographic terms, these are the individual 'parts' of light energy that radiate from every point of a subject. Light rays that enter the lens are bent, or refracted, so that they come into sharp focus precisely where the film is located, forming an image on the film.

'L'-shapes
A framing device made from two 'L'-shaped pieces of dark-coloured cardboard, which are used to make a picture frame shape. This composition aid allows you to preview how the final photograph will look.

M

Macro lens
A lens designed to allow closer-than-normal focusing so extreme close-up pictures can be taken.

Macro setting
A lens setting found on many SLR zoom lenses and some compacts. This allows the lens to focus on a single point that is closer than the normal focusing range of the lens.

Microprism collar
A focusing aid found in the centre of the viewfinder of many SLRs. It is a shimmering circular band, which clears when the lens is correctly focused.

N

Negative
A film image showing dark areas of the subject as light, and light areas as dark. In a colour negative, the colours will also be reversed. When printed, subject tones and colours appear normal.

O

Overexposure
This occurs when too much light reaches the film, giving a very light, bleached print.

P

Panorama
A picture made by taking overlapping images of a scene and then sticking them together to give a longer picture than would otherwise be possible.

Pentaprism
A five-sided prism inside an SLR camera. This corrects the inverted image so that it appears the right way round in the viewfinder.

Photographic paper
Paper coated with a light-sensitive emulsion, designed to reproduce a positive print from a film negative. Black and white printing paper is available in both resin-coated and fibre-based types. Resin-coated paper has a barrier under the emulsion that prevents chemicals and water penetrating into the paper itself. This makes processing and washing times much shorter than with fibre-based types, which become saturated. Although fibre-based papers take longer to process and wash, and tend to curl when drying, they do produce richer blacks and cleaner whites than resin-coated, papers so many photographers prefer them.

Photojournalism
Telling a story using pictures. Captions may be added but the photographs are the most important part.

Polarizing filter
A grey-coloured filter that, when fitted over the camera lens, removes some types of reflection, such as those from glass windows and the surface of water. It also tends to strengthen the colour of blue skies and so increase the contrast between sky and clouds.

R

Reflector
Any material, such as a piece of white cardboard, that reflects light onto the subject. Reflectors are usually positioned opposite the light source to reflect light back onto the subject, lightening the shadowy areas.

S

Safelight
A special red light that is used when making black-and-white prints. Black-and-white photographic printing paper is not sensitive to this colour, so you can work in the darkroom with some light on.

Self-timer
A control button that delays the shutter-release. This gives the photographer time to run around in front of the camera and be included in the picture. On most cameras, the delay is 10 seconds.

Shutter
A light-tight barrier, either in the lens or inside the camera body, that opens to allow light entering the lens to reach the film. The length of time the shutter stays open can be varied depending on the exposure needed by the film.

Shutter-release button
A control button found on all cameras. When pressed, the shutter opens, allowing light from the lens to reach the film.

Slide
A film image that shows subject tones and colours correctly. Prints can be made from slides, but usually they are meant to be projected onto a wall or screen for viewing. Slides are often called transparencies or positives.

Slow film
Film that reacts more slowly to light and is used when lighting conditions are bright. Slow films have small ISO numbers, such as ISO 100 or 200.

SLR
An abbreviation for single lens reflex. This type of camera has a lens that can be taken off and changed for another. An angled mirror inside the camera body reflects light from the lens up into the viewfinder, so that you always see the subject as the picture will eventually look.

Spiral
A plastic or stainless-steel spiral-

shaped device that holds an entire roll of exposed film. Once the film is loaded onto the spiral, it is inserted into a developing tank containing processing chemicals. The shape of the spiral ensures that the coils of film are kept well separated from each other so that the chemicals can reach all parts of the emulsion.

Split ring
A focusing aid found on some SLR cameras. When the image is properly focused, the two halves of the image within the ring match. When unfocused, they do not.

Sprocket holes
Holes running along the top and bottom of 35 mm film. Inside the camera, the film transport system has tiny 'teeth', which fit into the holes and move the film forwards and backwards from cassette to take-up spool.

Squeegee tongs
Plastic tongs lined with pads of foam rubber used to remove excess water from processed film.

Standard (or normal) lens
On a 35 mm camera, this is a lens with a focal length of about 50 mm. It is called a 'normal' lens because the angle of view, or amount of a scene it takes in, is about the same as you would see with the naked eye. A lens with a shorter focal length is known as a wide-angle; one with a longer focal length is called a telephoto.

Stop bath
A processing chemical used in the darkroom to process film and printing paper. It halts the action of developing solution.

T

Telephoto lens
On a 35 mm camera, this is a lens with a focal length greater than 50 mm. Telephotos have a narrow

angle of view and fill the frame with a small area of the subject. Telephoto lenses are very useful for sport, natural history, and candid photography.

Test strip
A strip of printing paper that has been subjected to a range of different exposures. These are produced either by altering the size of the aperture of the enlarger lens or, more usually, by altering the length of time the enlarger is switched on. A test strip may contain, for example, exposures of 5, 10, 15, and 25 seconds. Once it is processed, you can see which exposure time is best, and then make an enlargement of the entire negative using this exposure.

Tram lines
Long, straight scratches running down the length of a film. This type of problem usually occurs if there are tiny particles of grit on the film pressure plate of a camera. Each time you wind on, the film is dragged over this grit and so the scratch becomes longer and longer. To prevent this, clean the film pressure plate before loading each new film into the camera.

Tripod
An adjustable three-legged stand with a platform on top, which holds the camera securely. You usually use a tripod when you need to keep the camera really steady, such as with a slow shutter speed.

U

Ultraviolet (UV) filter
This colourless lens filter helps to remove excess amounts of UV light, which is often seen as a haze in the distance on landscape scenes and in coastal regions. Because it is colourless, many photographers leave a UV filter on the camera to protect the delicate front surface of the lens.

Underexposure
This occurs when too little light reaches the film, and gives very dark prints.

V

Viewfinder
The sighting device of a camera, which allows you to aim the camera lens accurately at the subject and to choose which parts of the subject will appear on the print.

Viewpoint
The position or angle of the camera when taking a photograph. Slight changes in camera viewpoint can make large differences to the appearance, not only of the subject itself, but also of its surroundings.

W

Wetting agent
A few drops of wetting agent, added to the final washing water of processed film, prevents droplets of water forming on the surface of the film as it dries. If left, these droplets can stain or mark the film.

Wide-angle lens
On a 35 mm camera, this is a lens with a focal length shorter than 50 mm. These lenses have a wide angle of view and take in a broad area of a scene, but the subject detail will look very small. They are useful lenses for panoramic scenes, and when working in cramped spaces where you can't move very far back from the subject.

Z

Zoom lens
This is a lens with an adjustable focal length, such as 28–70 mm or 70–210 mm. It can be used to produce a range of effects.

INDEX

Bold type indicates the main subject headings.

A

abstract images/designs 66, 78 – 79
action photography 44 – 47
add-on flash gun 15, **16**, 26, 27
animal photography 42 – 43, 48 – 49, 58
aperture 12, **13**, **21**, 43, 44, 76
  and focus 21
autoexposure **14**, 44
autofocus **14**, 33, 80
automatic film transport 14

B

backlighting 26, 27
baseboard 30, 78
black-and-white:
  negative film 18,19, 28, 29,
  prints 18, 19, 30 – 31
blurring 44, 61
books 87
bounced flash 27
buildings 50 – 51, 58
built-in flash 14, 15, 16, 26

C

cable release **16**, 76, 80, 81
camera:
  types of 14 –17
  using a 20 – 21, 32
camera obscura 12
camera shake 32
candid shots 38, 39, 56, 58
chemicals:
  for developing 28, 29
  for printing 30, 31
cityscapes 22, 60, 62
close-ups 55, 57, 76 – 77
colour:
  negative film 18,19
  prints 18, 19
  slides 19
compact cameras 13, **14**, **15**
  using 20
composition 22 – 23

converging verticals 50
cropping images 72

D

darkroom **28**, 30, 78
daylight-balanced film 62
depth of field 21, 43, 76
developer 28, 29, 30, 31
developing 28 – 29
developing tank 28, 29
diffused:
  flash 27
  light 40
diffusing material 27
direct flash 27
displaying photographs 84 – 86
disposable cameras 14
distorted images 66, 67

E

en (enlarged) prints 84
enlarger 30, 78
eyeline 42
exposure 12, 13, **21**, 24

F

f stops 21
family portraits 41
fast film 18
fault finder 32 – 35
feeding wildlife 49
fill-in flash 27
film 12, 13, 14, **18 –19**, 62
  construction of 28
  developing **28 – 29**
  exposure time 21
  loading/rewinding 34, 35
film cartridge 14, 18
film clip 28, 29
film image 12
film speed 18, **19**, 24
filter holder 75
filters 16, 75
fixed-focus **14**, 38
fixer 28, 29, 30, 31
flash gun, add- on 15, **16**, 26, 27
flash light 26 – 27
  and daylight 44

errors in the use of 34, 35
flash synchronization 34
floppy disk 17
focal lengths 16, 32
focus/focusing 12, **21**, 22, 33
focusing aid 21
fogging 34
frames, choice of 86
framing 86
  montage 68 – 69
  using L-shapes 84
framing (composition) 23, 71, 78
  errors 32
freezing 44, 61

G

gelatine special effect filters 75
grainy images 19
group portraits 41, 68

H

holiday photography 56 – 59
horizon line 60
hot shoe 16, 26

I

instant picture cameras *see*
  Polaroid cameras
ISO (International Standards
  Organization) 18, 19

L

L-shapes, framing with 84
landscape photography 22, 23, 24,
  60 – 61, 63
large format cameras 17, 18
lens 12, **13**, 15
  and autofocus 14
  and fixed-focus 14
  obstruction of 32
  see also aperture, macro lens,
  telephoto lens, wide-angle lens
  zoom lens
lens flare 33
light 12, 13, 19, 21
  see also natural light

M

macro lens 23, 48, 71, **76**
magazines 87
microprism collar 21
microscope adaptors 16
mirrors, using 81
montage 66 – 69
mounting 86

N

natural light 24 – 25, 40, 60, 70, 78
nature photography 48 – 49
  see also animal photography
negatives 28, 29
Niépce, Nicéphore 12

O

110 cameras/film 14, 18, 19
overlapping frames 34

P

panning 44, 45, 62
panoramas 14, 56, 64 – 65
panoramic cameras 62
parallax:
  error 20
  marks **20**, 32
people 38 – 39, 40 – 41, 52 – 53
  see also action photography,
  sport photography
personal view 52 – 53
photo albums 84
photo story 54 – 55
photocards 85
photograms 78
photographic exhibitions 87
photography clubs 87
photo-journalists 54
pinhole pictures 12
pivoting the camera 45, 62
point of focus 22, 23
Polaroid cameras 17, 18
portraits:
  of animals 42 – 43
  of people 38 – 39
  posed 38, 53
  self- 80 – 81
  using flash 27
printing paper 30, 31, 78
print tongs 30, 31
prints 18, 19
  displaying 84 – 86

framing 86
  making 30 – 31
processing errors 35
professional cameras 17

R

red eye 35
reflection 51, 74
reflector 40, 70

S

safelight 30
self-portraits 80 – 81
self-timer 80
shadows 24, 25, 60
sharp focus 21, 76
sheet film 18
shutter 12, **13**
shutter-release button 12, 13, 20, 80
shutter speed **21**
  and camera shake 32
  and close-ups 76
  and mirrors 81
  and moving water 61
  and sport/action photography 44,
  45, 46
silhouettes 25
silver salts 12, 19, 28
single lens reflex cameras *see*
  SLR cameras
slide film 18, 19
slow film 18, 19
SLR cameras 13, **15**
  using 21
soft-focus filter 75
special effects 74 – 75
split-ring 21
squeegee tongs 28, 29
still life 57, 70 – 73
still video camera 17
stop bath 28, 29, 30, 31
support, using a 20,
  and camera shake 32
  and panoramas 64
  and portrait shots 38
  see also tripod

T

telephoto lens 15, 16
  and animal/nature photography
  43, 48
  and camera shake 32
  and people photography 38, 39

35 mm cameras *see* compact
  cameras, SLR cameras
timer 29
tram lines 34
transparency film 18, 19
tripod 62, 64, 70, 76, 80, 81

U

useful addresses 87

V

viewfinder **12**, 13, 15, 80
  in compact cameras 20
  in SLR cameras 21
viewpoint **22**, 23, 46, 47
vignettes 33

W

water, photographing moving 61
waterproof case 16
weather 24 – 25, 60
wetting agent 29
wide-angle lens 15, **16**
  and animal photography 42
  and buildings 50
  and panoramas 62

Z

zoom lens 15, **16**
  and animal/nature photography
  43, 48
  and panoramas 62
  and people 38, 39, 56